EDUCATIONAL INCLUSION AS ACTION RESEARCH

INCLUSIVE EDUCATION

Series Editors:

Gary Thomas, Chair in Education, Oxford Brookes University, and
Christine O'Hanlon, School of Education, University of East Anglia

The movement towards inclusive education is gathering momentum throughout the world. But how is it realized in practice? The volumes within this series
will examine the arguments for inclusive schools and the evidence for the
success of inclusion. The intention behind the series is to fuse a discussion
about the ideals behind inclusion with pictures of inclusion in practice. The
aim is to straddle the theory/practice divide, keeping in mind the strong social
and political principles behind the move to inclusion while observing and
noting the practical challenges to be met.

Current and forthcoming titles:

Christine O'Hanlon: *Educational Inclusion as Action Research: An interpretive
   discourse*
Darshan Sachdev: *Inclusion at Large*
David Skidmore: *Inclusion: The Experience of Teachers and Parents*
Gary Thomas and Andrew Loxley: *Deconstructing Special Education and Con-
   structing Inclusion*
Gary Thomas and Mark Vaughan: *Inclusive Education – A Reader*
Carol Vincent: *Including Parents?*

EDUCATIONAL INCLUSION AS ACTION RESEARCH

An interpretive discourse

Christine O'Hanlon

Open University Press

Open University Press
McGraw-Hill Education
McGraw-Hill House
Shoppenhangers Road
Maidenhead
Berkshire
England
SL6 2QL

email: enquiries@openup.co.uk
world wide web: www.openup.co.uk

First published 2003

A catalogue record of this book is available from the British Library

ISBN 0 335 20732 4 (pb)   0 335 20733 2 (hb)

Library of Congress Cataloging-in-Publication Data
CIP data applied for

Typeset by RefineCatch Limited, Bungay, Suffolk
Printed in the UK by Bell & Bain Ltd, Glasgow

I wish to dedicate this book to my grandson Ben who has provided a healthy and active respite for me from writing. He has reminded me about the most important things of value in life.

Contents

Series editors' preface

'Inclusion' has become something of an international buzz-word. It's difficult to trace its provenance or the growth in its use over the last two decades, but what is certain is that it is now *de rigeur* for mission statements, political speeches and policy documents of all kinds. It has become a cliché – obligatory in the discourse of all right-thinking people.

The making of 'inclusion' into a cliché, inevitable as it perhaps is, is nevertheless disappointing, since it means that the word is often merely a filler in the conversation. It means that people can talk about 'inclusion' without really thinking about what they mean, merely to add a progressive gloss to what they are saying. Politicians who talk casually about the need for a more inclusive society know that they will be seen as open-minded and enlightened, and will be confident in the knowledge that all sorts of difficult practical questions can be circumvented. If this happens, and if there is insufficient thought about the nitty gritty mechanics (what the Fabians called 'gas and water' matters), those who do work hard for inclusion can easily be dismissed as peddling empty promises.

This series is dedicated to examining in detail some of the ideas which lie behind inclusive education. Inclusion, much more than 'integration' or 'mainstreaming', is embedded in a range of contexts – political and social as well as psychological and educational – and our aim in this series is to make some examination of these contexts. In providing a forum for discussion and critique we hope to provide the basis for a wider intellectual and practical foundation for more inclusive practice in schools and elsewhere.

In nothing that inclusive education is indeed about more than simply 'integration', it is important to stress that inclusive education is really about extending the comprehensive ideal in education. Those who talk about it are therefore less concerned with children's supposed 'special educational needs' (and it is becoming increasingly difficult meaningfully to define what such needs are) and more concerned with developing an education system in which tolerance, diversity and equity are striven for. To aim for such developments is surely uncontentious; what is perhaps more controversial is the means by which this is done. There are many and varied ways of helping to develop more inclusive schools and the authors of this series look at some of these. While one focus in this has to be on the place and role of the special school, it is by no means the only focus: the thinking and practice which go on inside and outside schools may do much to exclude or marginalize children and the authors of this series try to give serious attention to such thinking and practice.

The books in this series therefore examine a range of matters: the knowledge of special education; the frames of analysis which have given legitimacy to such knowledge; the changing political mood which inspires a move to inclusion. In the context of all this, they also examine some new developments in inclusive thinking and practice inside and outside schools. *Deconstructing Special Education and Constructing Inclusion*, one of the first books in this series, looks both backwards and forwards. Back, to the intellectual schemas within which special education was built, and forward to the kind of education appropriate for the inclusive society for which many people are striving. It is critical of the thinking of the past, while taking seriously the changes presented by inclusive ideals.

Gary Thomas
Christine O'Hanlon

Acknowledgements

I began thinking about this book some time ago, when professional development courses I taught were widening access to include a broad range of professionals, beyond teachers. There were psychologists, paramedics, local education authority officers, headteachers, special educational needs co-ordinators, classroom assistants and many other education-related personnel, who were motivated to extend and develop their expertise for more inclusive practices. I have also worked with some inspiring and dedicated colleagues in schools and universities who have broadened my field of vision. I cannot forget the pupils, children, young people, aspiring teachers, students and adult learners who struggled to make a path for themselves by exploring beneath the surface. I am grateful to them all for teaching me so much and providing a rich resource of stories for my teaching and writing. They form a multicultural group from Ireland to Asia. Some of their stories I recollect and include in this book.

I am grateful to the following teachers for their direct contributions to this book: Linda Hothersall, Rosemary Williams and Andrea Fulton. Thanks are also due to countless teachers and associated educational professionals who have taken in the past, and are currently taking, master's and doctoral courses for inclusive practice. They have enriched their institutions and cultures by their informed understanding and applied research expertise.

Prologue

This journey is required
– here you come face to face
with the petrific mace
which can never explain these rocks
– black diorite?
They're polished like ice
how can we have gone below the surface
to find only a deeper surface?

(Paulin 2002)

I begin this book by sharing some of my biography, which has pointed me in the particular direction of resolving professional inclusion issues in schools through action research. The biographical theme within practitioner research is one that is increasingly relevant to the understanding of how we learn and use educational theories and ideas.

I was educated in Northern Ireland. I have been educated through exposure to an eclectic range of theories and ideas, many of which are not directly connected with education. I attended a Catholic primary school and later a convent grammar school, both of which were partly government financed and open to all pupils, including non-Catholics, except those with obvious disabilities. There was a wide range of pupil ability in both schools but no extra support for pupils with manifest learning disabilities. Children who arrived from other countries were immersed into the classroom culture and expected to fit in as far as possible. Ethnic minority groups were not visible or identified, because there were so few, except perhaps for children from traveller families. I then progressed to university in the 1960s, where I graduated with a bachelor of arts and became a teacher. At that time prospective teachers either trained for a postgraduate certificate in education for a year or undertook a two-year induction period in school, when school inspectors made regular progress reports about their practical expertise. I chose the latter course of action. I didn't immediately undertake formal teacher training and learned to survive on my wits. I initially became a teacher like the teachers I knew. I modelled myself on those teachers who influenced me most and I tried my best to emulate them. My first permanent teaching position was at a school for boys aged from 4 to 16 years, which was designated as a school for 'mal-adjusted and educationally sub-normal pupils'. Today it would be termed a school for boys with 'emotional and behaviour disturbance, and learning dif-ficulties'. I felt the teaching role was a challenge for me and I was determined to make a success of it. The pupils were disturbed and disturbing in various ways, and to begin with I was a very traditional teacher. After about nine to twelve months at the school I thought, 'Am I providing the best possible learning environment, opportunities and curriculum for my pupils?' I had doubts about using a traditional academic curriculum with these pupils and wanted to find interesting activities that would motivate them and engage them in active learning. It was left to me to decide on what, when and how the pupils were to be taught (with the headteacher's approval). I was allowed to experiment and evaluate pupils' progress how I chose. There was a sense of freedom and choice in the role, which suited me well and encouraged my artistic leanings, a very different situation from today's specified curriculum. However, there were days during that first year at the school when the act of facing the pupils demanded great courage, because the job challenged all my personal resources. I found it difficult to merge the different perspectives of caring, teaching and classroom management. Nevertheless, I prepared my lessons well, and I concentrated on a varied and diverse curriculum, which emphasized literacy development, art and drama. My main aim with the pupils was to develop their literacy skills and to prepare them for independent living at 16 plus.

Department of Education inspectors came to the classroom regularly to appraise my teaching skills during that period. I felt that the inspections were unreal, because they seemed to have little or no relationship to the com-plexities of the situation that I was struggling with. My teaching was being evaluated rather than supported. Inspections often occurred in the afternoon, when the pupils were more disturbed, or disturbing, than usual, and the time was given up to the observation of my teaching, which became surreal and unnatural. This situation seemed to unsettle the pupils more than usual, because the inspector moved around the classroom 'observing', having in-depth discussions with me and distracting me from giving the pupils the attention they demanded. I felt that judgements were being made about the teaching against some unseen criteria, which I could not access because of their invisibility.

However, the visits made it clear to me that teaching these pupils in the segregated context in which they were placed was 'new', unexplored territory for the teaching profession. It was a 'segregated' context because it was a school that only accepted pupils who had been referred via the psychological services for 'special' and separate education, which differed from the normal primary or secondary schooling.

Teaching these pupils required creative thinking and skills that could not simply be passed on from person to person. The school was staffed by teachers who were trained for either primary or secondary schools, because at that time there was no specific training for special education. After observing my colleagues in the school, I realized that what worked for the older male teachers didn't work for me; what worked for the women teachers with younger pupils didn't apply because many pupils were transferred to the school and to my class at secondary transfer stage at eleven years. I had to figure out for myself what was appropriate in the classroom from abstract professional theories and principles that I had gleaned in my psychology course at university. The teaching was challenging and tiring, but if I wanted to continue to teach pupils with educational differences something had to change. After some deliberation it became evident that it wasn't just the pupils who were problematic. There were social dynamics in the classroom and school that affected both pupils and teachers. A dynamic energy came with the pupils, affected their interactions and changed from day to day. The static charges from person to person were felt and experienced by everyone, and my responses to them were intuitive rather than reasoned. To begin to improve the situation, I focused on myself as the first person to transform and change. I was having problems teaching these pupils. I thought I was a very dedicated teacher, but the classroom was often tense, and 'outbursts' from pupils were never far away. I had to be prepared to deal with all kinds of pupil behaviour, regardless of what caused it.

I decided that I was trying too hard. Perhaps I was worrying too much about the pupils' literacy skills and their academic ability. Perhaps I was a little afraid of them. The pupils frequently behaved in unexpected and uncontrolled ways, they were aggressive with each other and many of them had been physically, emotionally or sexually abused. I realized that I was quite disturbed by a number of the pupils' home lives and the conditions they experienced beyond the school gates. I realized that I would have to come to terms with their disturbing behaviour and its unsettling effects on me to become a better teacher, but I had no way of knowing how to do that.

I felt that the teaching I had known, and was modelling, was essentially academic and examination focused, yet these pupils faced no examinations in the future; what they needed was an all-round education for their survival in later life. How was I to meet the educational needs of pupils with educational differences, a diversity of personalities and complex emotional needs? I decided that I was being too academic in my teaching focus and aims. I tried to see the pupils more as interesting people rather than as learners with differences. Until then, I had been seeing them only as learners who reflected my successful or unsuccessful teaching through their successful or unsuccessful learning. If I was to see them as real people, perhaps I could succeed in teaching them and also help them with their social and emotional difficulties. I began, quite intuitively, an action research process. The first thing I did – as we also do in action research – was to observe the pupils in the learning environment. I noticed that the first few minutes each day in the classroom were crucial to pupils' attitudes and class harmony for the rest of the day. Facing schoolwork immediately on entry to the classroom was causing problems for many pupils. There was a struggle against pupil resistance, which was unproductive for all concerned. After discussion with colleagues, I decided that, instead of settling pupils into schoolwork straight from the bus in the morning, I would bring them into the classroom and allow them to relax and choose whatever classroom activities they wished. Games and toys were left on desks and on the floor for their use. During this time, I walked around the room and talked to them. It was usually in the first 45 minutes that pupils who were upset and disturbed coming to school could be identified and helped. Some of the boys had come straight from their beds without any breakfast, completing their dressing on the bus. In easing up on academic activities at the beginning of the school day, I was able to pick up who was in a particularly unsettled emotional state and who wasn't, and how pupils were relating to each other and to me. I was also able to show some concern for them, by listening to them and getting to know them better and valuing their experiences. I changed my daily priority from facilitating curriculum knowledge and information, to show that I accepted them as individuals with moods and feelings. I didn't just appreciate them because they were good at learning whatever I was teaching, or had specific skills in responding to the curriculum taught. I encouraged them to demonstrate their skills and talents for their peers and discovered that many of them were accomplished in music, singing, art and football. I would never have known, valued or capitalized on pupils' hidden strengths without the space to observe, reflect and discuss evidence with colleagues.

Things seemed to start happening after these changes were implemented. A calm atmosphere descended on the classroom within a very short period. One pupil was seen regularly to hide in the cloakroom rather than go home on the school bus. Parents were seen dropping off children at the school gates, saying, 'He missed the bus but he insisted on coming to school.' When local teacher training colleges sent students to the school to observe practice, the students asked over and over again, 'What's happening in this classroom? What's going on?' They wanted to emulate the classroom practice and wanted the rationale for success with the pupils to be explained. I was unable to explain the practice fully without bringing in the personal reflection, change, values, attitudes, thinking and action that influenced my professional practice.

Learning became more of a fun activity for the pupils, and games were devised for the core activities involving mathematics and literacy. Everyone contributed to the creation of learning games, which were used only for as long as they worked. The games routines were rotated to ensure that interest levels remained high. Colleagues showed an interest in what was happening and spent time simply observing the classroom routines and practice.

After many years of teaching at this school and supporting student teachers on 'teaching practice' in the classroom, I took up an appointment as a lecturer in higher education and became a teacher-trainer. In this new context I found myself again attempting to develop and evaluate my teaching. One aspect of my role in higher education involved supervising and supporting student teachers in the classroom. In this role I could integrate modelling behaviour, theory and practice. I encouraged student teachers to reflect on their own strengths and to model themselves on teachers they had known, only when they found that it suited their character, the pupils and the school ethos and context. Simply modelling the current behaviour of classroom teachers didn't seem to me to be the right approach for trainee teachers.

At the same time, I was teaching educational psychology and philosophy courses, because I had studied these subjects for my initial degree. I outlined educational theories related to teaching and learning for initial teacher training and postgraduate certificate in education students. I presented ideas in a critical manner because I always reviewed evidence and research to support a perspective from both ends of a theoretical continuum, examining both the antithesis and the thesis. There were always opposing educational theories about what was best in classrooms, how children learned and what teaching was all about. I believed it was both an intellectual exercise and a challenge to decide for oneself what was best in individual educational situations.

Yet the teachers and student teachers I taught inevitably said to me, 'What do *you* think? What do *you* do?' I replied, 'Are you really interested in what I do?' They said, 'We want to know exactly what you would do in this situation.' This surprised me because I thought that only 'big name' theories and ideas were important to students and teachers. That began another reflective learning phase in my professional life. Until then, I had proposed idealistic textbook theories to students. Their questions prompted me to look even more closely at my own particular practice. I started to bring in photographs and other evidence of my teaching, and when I looked at it closely, in retrospect, I realized that my practice wasn't as idealistic as I thought it was. In fact, my practice was a lot more directed and controlling than I ever believed. I had always talked about pupil freedom, creativity and putting pupil needs first, but in reality, when I examined my everyday teaching, it was also very organized and very controlling. This had many positive aspects, as pupils clearly experienced increased self-esteem and stability. However, the downside was that I could never leave the room or go for a coffee, because whenever I left the room, or was absent for any reason, the pupils would act aggressively and destructively in the classroom. I realized that there was such stability and order in the classroom organization if I changed the arrangements for the day, the pupils would become confused or act up. However, it wasn't just the order that made a difference to them. It was also the manner of interaction with them, which was always respectful, interested and humorous, through the curriculum games and play focus. Everything stopped when pupils' personal needs signalled attention, and all problems were resolved within the classroom through discussion and talk rather than punishment or exclusion.

In the higher education context I also realized that teaching, whether it was with children or adults, was a very personally interactive and emotionally satisfying occupation for me. It was really through these challenges to me as a practitioner, rather than as an academic, that I started to reflect about where I was and what I wanted to achieve through my professional role.

I became the director of a full-time course for serving teachers of pupils with learning difficulties in mainstream primary, secondary and special schools. They were then called 'remedial' teachers. Traditionally, teaching in higher education institutions was transmission teaching, lecturing or tell-and-sell.

Teachers and educational professionals were signing up for in-service courses and expecting to be inculcated with current educational theories and practices, but I wanted to examine exactly where *they* were in the reality of schooling. I encouraged them to talk about their teaching. They responded by talking about what they thought they did. So we asked the question, 'What is really going on here? How do we obtain evidence? How can we check it out?'

I wasn't in a position to go into their classrooms and watch them teach. I didn't feel it was appropriate, because it was each teacher's responsibility to make a difference to their own pupils within the specific context and environment of their own classrooms and schools. These were often very different, depending on the school's location, ethos and aims, whether they were rural, urban, special or mainstream. However, it was essential to begin by challenging the teachers about what their professional needs were at the outset of their learning, and what they hoped to gain from the course. They began by taking the first day to think about, and explain, why they had signed up to the course. They outlined what their problems and difficulties were in their schools and classrooms. They reflected about what they wanted to gain from their in-service experience, and how they could obtain evidence to prove a need for change and improvement.

They all agreed that these questions were best answered by spending time in their own schools and classrooms. After negotiation and discussion with the course group, it was agreed that they spend one day a week investigating their current school practice. The teachers planned, through weekly research methods sessions and discussion, how best to spend their time, to record the school or work situation and to report back to the group about the outcomes. They selected individualized investigative means to suit their chosen research focus, so as to uncover contradictions and hidden assumptions in school practice, through photography, video/audio recording, note taking, observation, document review, interviews and the implementation of specific teaching programmes with selected pupils. Each week they brought back the evidence to share with teachers on the course, to discuss what their problems and difficulties were, what the evidence was, what it meant to them and what they needed to change for better practice in teaching and learning. They negotiated their own group rules for democratic organization and feedback to ensure confidentiality and anonymity through discussion. This was a unique opportunity for them to do something in their schools and classrooms without the constant everyday pressure that made them too busy to reflect on what was taking place.

At about the same time as I was doing this, I was reading and absorbing ideas from humanist psychology, philosophy, sociology and action research. I realized I had at last found a label for what I had been doing, because I couldn't 'name' the kind of practice that the teachers were developing on this particular course. 'Action research' was the term that suited this particular methodological approach, because it was teacher-centred, formative and involved self-evaluation. It was also a means of developing professional self-knowledge and creating practitioner theories about teaching and learning. I began to understand the ideas behind action research, through reading

(Kemmis and McTaggart 1981; Elliott 1981, 1985; Elliott and Ebbutt 1985), which then became a way of life for myself and many of the teachers with whom I worked.

When experienced teachers choose to advance and improve their teaching practice through professional development courses, they can choose different learning approaches to suit themselves. One approach is to employ inter- pretive discourse to share professional concerns and to evaluate professional practice with colleagues. This is the practice of collaborating with research participants or professional colleagues, not necessarily working in the same institution, to investigate, discuss, debate and challenge current educational practice. The group process of interpretive discourse, which I came to see as a central feature of action research, recognizes teachers as individuals with many voices. Interpretive discourse gives group members an opportunity to reflect in a supportive and collaborative manner, and provides a learning environment that is safe for individuals to formulate, challenge and develop their ideas. Implicit in this process is both a personal and professional trans- formation for participants because there is no *professional* development without *personal* development. The two features are so closely aligned that they cannot be separated (O'Hanlon 1993).

Initial teacher training programmes currently on offer in the UK are more comprehensive, intensive and supportive of teachers at the start of their teaching careers than in the past. I offer my personal account simply to show how action research evolved for one person as a basis for professional life. The themes inherent in the autobiographical account are the core themes of this book and will be developed in the following chapters. They are:

- perceiving a need for change;
- demonstrating a willingness to involve oneself in evaluation and reflective appraisal of situations;
- providing evidence about unsatisfactory or problematic practice;
- discussing issues and concerns with colleagues;
- using action research for inclusion as a democratic and inclusive process of enquiry;
- employing interpretive discourse in collecting evidence and discussion;
- becoming reflexive and self-evaluative through the research process;
- recording both personal and professional change;
- producing a case record for public access and dissemination.

CHAPTER ONE

Policy, social justice and inclusion

An education system appropriate to the demands of the twenty-first century must be designed to establish a foundation of knowledge and skill for all children and to nurture the particular talents of each child.

(Social Justice Commission 1994: 131)

Within all contemporary societies there are groups that struggle to gain equality of opportunity and social justice in national educational systems. Research has shown that education systems can be key in perpetuating or curtailing educational disadvantages for marginalized individuals and groups (e.g. Troyna and Hatcher 1992; Foster *et al.* 1996). There has also been extensive critical debate about the effects of special education on its pupils (e.g. Slee 1996; Pijl *et al.* 1997; Vlachou 1997), while the effects of educational disadvantage and underperformance have been well documented (Tomlinson 2000).

In 1994 the UK government commissioned a report on social justice (Social Justice Commission 1994), which uncovered an uncomfortable situation. Despite 50 years of educational reform, the education system continued to fail the great majority of children. Even today, the UK has the lowest level of educational provision for under-5s in the European Union, while the average state primary class size is 27 pupils (DfES 2002). In private schools the ratio is halved. Despite government attempts to raise participation, only two in five of Britain's 19-year-olds is still in full-time education (YCS 2001) and, disturbingly, two-thirds of school leavers reported their main immediate destination to be employment (HESA 2001). Universities are still mainly accessed by pupils from economically advantaged families and private schools, and recent proposals to increase fees for university education are unlikely to reverse this trend. In the first decade of the twenty-first century, a person's life chances are even more powerfully affected by their education than in the past. People with no qualifications are more likely to be out of work, and the earnings gap between those with a university degree, or its equivalent, and those without is growing wider. Yet politicians continue to assert the values of social justice: the equal worth of all citizens, their equal right to be able to meet their basic needs, the need to spread opportunities and life chances as widely as possible and the reduction and elimination of unjustified inequalities. This is to be attained through priorities for government policy, which include:

- universal pre-school education;
- basic skills for all children through literacy and numeracy targets in the National Curriculum;
- high achievement for all young people through a unified qualifications system for 14- to 19-year-olds;
- training investment by employers;
- the expansion of university education;
- the development of lifelong learning opportunities.

Education and skills are seen as the route to opportunity, employability and security. Yet, as the Social Justice Commission recognized back in 1994, a person's individual attributes and resources are not the only factor to affect educational opportunities and life chances. Where a person lives, who they live with and how that community generally lead their lives can be as important as one's personal resources. 'Social capital' is identified as the key to success in communities. This consists of the means to access 'networks, norms and trust that facilitate co-ordination and co-operation for mutual benefit' (Putnamm 1993). A healthy society depends on its social capital, as a good in itself, and to make life possible.

The challenge today lies in building social capital and social well-being in a fragmented and struggling school system. What must be recognized is that there are immeasurable benefits to be gained from what people give to each other, pupil to pupil, pupil to teacher, parent to teacher and teacher to pupil, in an interactive mainstream school environment. Yet such covert rewards are rarely used as an argument to support mainstream education because of their invisibility. As educators we need to be aware of what children with special needs, language and cultural differences contribute to a school community. This is an under-researched area and discussion all too readily focuses upon pupils' needs rather than their added value to education in specific school communities.

The political climate currently favours the principle of inclusion and education for an inclusive society, and the failure of many schools to educate and include all children is recognized. The aim is now to create an education system that will develop the potential of all children in society and recognize and value their differences. If pupils are not included in mainstream education then they will be denied a rounded and inclusive educational experience.

Schooling never was intended to educate the majority of pupils. There is a notional 20 per cent of pupils with special educational needs (SEN) in England and Wales proposed by the Warnock Committee (DES 1978) and an unknown percentage of students from ethnic/cultural minorities, non-English speaking backgrounds and disadvantaged social communities who have found the school system inadequate for their needs. The idea of inclusion may be illusory (Ainscow 1999) or it may be a profoundly subversive and transformational undertaking, overhauling traditional forms of schooling (Slee 1999).

Links to social justice issues

Discussion about the aims of education in any school setting frequently uses such concepts as 'freedom', 'equality', 'justice', 'personal autonomy', 'self-realization' and 'the growth of understanding'. Yet these educational values are notoriously vague and cannot be clarified by being broken down into concrete quantifiable indicators of educational outcomes. They are qualities to be realized in the way teachers interact with and treat their pupils in learning situations, rather than extrinsic products of such interactions in either special or mainstream schools. To say that a learning situation is 'free', 'equal' and 'just', or that it enables pupils to 'learn autonomously' or 'realize themselves', is to say something about the nature of the conditions for learning established by the teacher, rather than its products. Therefore, teaching is seen as an ethical activity, and an appropriate focus for practical investigation and reflection. All areas of education and schooling are open to scrutiny in the advancement of such values and concepts within inclusive practice through research processes like action research. However, it is argued that, within a discourse of ethics, 'maintaining segregated special education is incompatible with the establishment of an equitable education system and hence, ultimately with an equitable society. It follows therefore that only inclusive education can deliver social justice' (Dyson 1999).

Rawls (1971) provides an important resource for thinking about the problems of justice because he balances the twin principles of equity and difference. The balance involves the equal distribution of social goods unless unequal distribution benefits people who are underprivileged, when 'more resources might be spent on the education of the less, rather than the more intelligent, at least in the early years of schooling'. Because inequalities of birth and natural endowment are undeserved, these inequalities should be compensated for by giving more attention to those with fewer natural assets and to those born into less favourable positions. As regards the principle of difference, it is aimed at improving 'the long-term expectation of the least favoured'. Within this principle is the notion of fraternity and enhanced self-respect, of which the latter is referred to as a 'primary good' that everyone needs (similar to social capital). Consequently, educational resources are to be distributed 'according to their worth in enriching the personal and social life of citizens'.

These ideas have not gone unchallenged (Young 1990). The basic criticism is that the disadvantaged are identified in terms of the relatively low share of social goods they possess. The task of eliminating identified disadvantages is then implemented by various compensatory social programmes, educational and otherwise. All are conceived and developed with little input from those most affected. This makes it profoundly undemocratic, because it assumes that social goods to be distributed, as well as the procedures by which this has to occur, are uncontroverted. They reflect the interests and values of those who have been, and continue to be, in charge. For example, consider a mainly Christian religious curriculum, which will not be improved by giving more help to religious minorities to master it in order to remove their perceived disadvantage.

Instead of using equality as a principle of rational distribution, there is a move towards equality as a principle of democratic distribution. In this 'participatory paradigm' the requirements of distributive justice and those of democracy are integrated – justice requires giving everyone an effective voice in negotiating goods and defining their own needs, particularly members of groups who have been historically excluded. The distributivist paradigm fits naturally with a top-down, expert-driven model of research. Administrators look for the misdistribution of goods, define group needs and then formulate the policies and practices to be implemented – and this is done in the name of equality. However, this model, like the distributivist paradigm with which it is associated, is both undemocratic and unjust.

The participatory paradigm, however, fits quite naturally with a model of research in which equality is sought not solely in the distribution of this or that predetermined good, but through the status and voice of the participants. Goods, along with needs, policies and practices, are negotiated and investigated in collaboration, with democracy and justice functioning as the overarching ideals – the ideals that underlie participatory action research.

The principle of difference is also found in Stenhouse's argument for a balance between a curriculum that provides all pupils with equal access to cultural goods, and a curriculum organized for the purposes of productive enterprise. Those with natural abilities suited to these purposes will achieve more than other pupils, but it may well benefit all pupils in the longer term.

> Arrangements in the educational system which distribute rewards and benefits unequally but justifiably in favour of the well-endowed should not disadvantage the less well-endoweds' equal access to the general culture.
>
> (Stenhouse 1975: 118)

Such access is seen as a necessary condition for acquiring self-esteem as a member of society, which is an essential primary good (Elliott 1998). However, access to the educational goods of society are controlled through educational policy and practice. It is only by making changes to the existing educational and institutional hegemony that wider access to 'primary goods' through inclusive practice can be attained. In past decades research on such matters carried out by positivist scientists looked at education as if it were a concrete system, which rendered pupils, teachers and other professionals as pawns, ever subject to the influences of predetermined forces in society. (Bogdan and Biklin 1982; Kincheloe 1991). Educational knowledge obtained through such methods was unhelpful to practitioners and misleading, because it attempted to erase the moral dimension of education, which is so evident in discussions related to 'justice' and 'inclusion'.

In recent years, however, there have been moves to redress past mistakes through the development of more democratic and inclusive research methods to influence educational practice. New forms of research developed in a post-modern idiom recognize that researchers should understand that their actions have multiple meanings. They realize that in carrying out their research they are not fully in control of the results of their actions. For example, in undertaking research to overcome what we recognize as oppressive educational practice, researchers risk bestowing power upon themselves by the very act of assuming the researcher's role. We must be aware that power can just as easily be identified in the forces of liberation as it can in the forces of repression and exploitation. The notions of equality, freedom and justice are ideas that become defined through the situations they are played out in. The dialogue would be very one sided if liberation was 'done' for, or 'to', others, even in the name of freedom. Research that is collaborative, inclusive and democratic encourages its participants to consider meanings in terms of the relationships of the struggle with its participants and within the dialogue constructed with them. Any research investigation should be critical of, and concerned with, deconstructing authoritative voices, those who speak for and on behalf of others. This includes the researchers deconstructing their own voices to critique their personal perceptions and explanations of what counts as inclusive practice. New interpretations are thereby created through the investigation of practices related to the historical and traditional meanings of everyday life in schools. However, all written reports of research findings are open to reinterpretation by their readers, including this text and the many texts that will be created in response to the impetus for inclusive practice in schools.

Inequality in educational practice has met with political pressure for its eradication. Academic educationalists have been instrumental in these initiatives over recent decades. Sociologists in particular have been effective in breaking down beliefs about differences in pupil ability or intelligence, with previous imputations about links between cultural deprivation and working-class homes. It is now understood that there is little or no evidence of real or relevant differences among children *per se*; instead, a social construction of schooling functions to serve the powerful interests of the schools, the state and the dominant classes and powerful groups in society. A new ideology, referred to as 'social constructivism', operates to show the socially constructed nature of school experience, exposing the pernicious influence of testing and assessment in special education, and the virus of sexism and racism in both mainstream and special education. However, this new position is not without its problems, because researchers still construct the events they investigate and are implicitly influenced by the social and educational contexts in which they operate. Much research to date on educational practice and pedagogy, other than practitioner research, has been unreflective about the way in which the researcher is associated with the research issue under investigation. How researchers relate to a social or educational problem, their means of investigation, their perceptions, explanations and analysis of evidence, are themselves social processes with a social product. This is an area where researchers need to be more self-consciously reflexive in the future (Foster *et al.* 1996). The process outlined in this book aims to encourage such reflexivity.

Justice and equity are not the only considerations that impinge on children's and young people's educational opportunities. Other factors include inclusive schooling, options within the curriculum, teaching quality and methods, respecting and valuing difference, maintaining communities and the creation of a reflexive investigative teaching profession. Inclusion and its practice is open to scrutiny in all areas and action research provides an agency for its practical interpretation and evaluation.

What is inclusion?

Inclusion suggests that no child or young person should be excluded from mainstream schooling because of perceived learning differences, language, cultural, racial, class, religious or behavioural differences. However, the reality is that many children and young people are segregated or excluded because they are seen to challenge the curriculum, academic outcomes and management strategies of mainstream classrooms and schools. Inclusion is not simply about making a decision between pupil placement in a mainstream versus a special school. There is a wide spectrum of inclusive practice, which may include placement in a special school for a short or longer period of time, for part of a day or week. Time spent at a special school should depend on the child's needs for a more specialized, specific or individual programme of care and education, which may be temporary or permanent.

Inclusion can be many things. It is a construct of the times in which we live and as such is a current politically correct ideology towards which there is an explicit progression in educational organizations and institutions nationally and internationally. This is based on the basic human need to embrace diverse human cultures and the religious, ethnic, differently focused and talented groups that make up a cohesive and educated society. Inclusion is a process of creating, through educational practice, diverse participation in all dynamic aspects of social and educational life. It means that schooling, which is part of the educative process of our culture, if it is to become fully inclusive, needs to become more flexible in terms of widening access, diversity and choice in the curriculum. Enabling all children to access the possibilities of achieving their potential, developing their talents and contributing what they have to give to the world requires inclusive practices. Restrictions or constraints of any kind on the natural curiosity and the urge to learn that everyone possesses from birth, often affect lifelong perceptions and attitudes. Special schooling for a small percentage of our children benefits them educationally in terms of more intensive and specialist teaching, different curricula and interaction with a smaller select group of peers. Although there is always the necessity for such schooling to be selective in terms of pupil intake and teaching and learning priorities, there is also the need to develop inclusive practices.

The state-supported school system is multicultured and multiethnic, and contains a melting pot of dynamism that comes from the diversity of the environments in which pupils live and schools are situated. Schools that are highly selective do not allow for the development of community in the context of a local neighbourhood. Selective schools create their own community in a non-locational sense, with people from diverse neighbourhoods. However, a child's social identity develops out of the membership of at least one group. Pupils attending their local school, situated in the community, benefit by participating in local community life and forming friendships and alliances with neighbourhood children and staff. Local community issues are learned through contacts with neighbours, and a sense of citizenship and civic responsibility develops from the 'in-group' solidarity of a school community. This is, however, not the experience of all pupils of school age. The concept of inclusion offers the possibility of going beyond traditional liberal values to stress the bonds that tie people together in communities. They are a matter not simply of tolerating social and educational differences but of recognizing each other's individual worth as community members who enrich communities by their contributions to them. Inclusion is about balancing the sectorial interests of community members through democratic negotiation and the fair, and possibly uneven, distribution of resources.

Terminology and labels

It is acknowledged that pupils *with* special educational needs (SEN), statemented pupils, pupils with emotional and behaviour disturbance (EBD) and other labels and syndromes, and pupils *from* many minority communities, are increasingly participating in mainstream schools (CSIE 1989). Inclusion and its practice is a political and ideological construct that needs to be interpreted through its demonstration in the real world of the classroom and school. Its rationale forms an uneven continuum of implementation, from mere social association to total immersion of pupils in mainstream classes and curricula. The range of possible opportunities for social and educational inclusion is considerable, yet they depend on the creativity and ingenuity of everyone involved in the care and education of children and young people. The change in terminology in recent years from 'integration' to 'inclusion' is not in itself enough to guarantee radical changes in traditional teaching procedures in mainstream schools to accommodate the educational needs of *all* pupils. The term 'integration' is often used in international contexts to refer to increased participation in ordinary schools, but generally the literature shows little consensus on the precise meanings of 'integration', 'inclusion' and 'mainstreaming' (Booth and Ainscow 1998). The concept of 'inclusion' is both illusory and evolving. Changes in pedagogy will define it in educational contexts. However, the role of education in influencing and making changes in society is not yet fully understood. It was Bernstein (1971) who first noted that 'Education cannot compensate for society', because it appeared to be reproducing rather than removing social inequalities. Moreover, the term special educational needs might itself be seen as a euphemism for the failure of schools to meet the educational needs of all their pupils (Barton 1987). When the SEN focus in education moved away from child-centred problems in the 1970s to focus more upon problems in schools, the environment and the social context, a greater responsibility was placed on mainstream teachers and schools to adapt and change to meet each pupil's needs. This movement has made the inclusion agenda explicit in educational policy directives and open to general public debate.

Inclusion is educating all children together in their local neighbourhood schools. It is offering a fully resourced school support service to all children whose families and carers wish them to be educated alongside their family, peers and local community. Inclusion is using the same generous resources that exist in 'special education' to enable the participation of pupils from special schools in mainstream schools. Inclusion may be partial or total, but often it is 'integration' struggling to be more inclusive. Integration is the process of assimilation of previously excluded individuals and groups of pupils into mainstream, or ordinary, schooling. 'Inclusion' has been aligned with the notion of assimilation, where the necessary school and curriculum adaptation and change are aimed at more equal provision, practice and support for marginalized individuals and groups of pupils. Inclusion implies a deliberate look at the school provision for all pupils and how it can be appropriately applied and adapted for pupils with learning or additional differences.

Pupils with educational or learning differences exist in every classroom or school, often without being officially identified. In the UK, the formal identification of different learning needs gives the statutory right for a pupil to be 'statemented'. The statementing procedure may be initiated by the parent or by the school (with children of school age) before decisions are made about the kind of education to be received by the child. A new Code of Practice has been approved (SU 2002), which requires that maintained schools and local education authorities (LEAs) attend to the latest statutory guidance from the Department for Education and Skills (DfES) on the practical operation of the new statutory framework for inclusion. When a child is 'statemented' there are certain legal obligations on the LEA and school to provide for the child's educational needs. However, it is possible that the parent or the school may not choose to take action as recommended by the LEA, e.g. the child may be removed from the present school and relocated to a private school, or to home tuition. When a child is 'statemented' a psychologist might assess the child, along with the teachers, parents and others connected with his or her health and education. The 'statement' subsequently produced becomes a legal obligation for those responsible for the child's educational needs. Without a 'statement' the child may be educated wherever he or she is accepted, and no specific legal obligation is put upon his or her educators to provide specialized teaching, learning support or other assistance. This is often the case for many children attending private schools or receiving alternative forms of education.

The professed aim of designating children as 'special' or 'different', when they are experiencing school-related difficulties, is to provide them with a better educational environment. The mainstream classroom is a setting where different learning environments can be created to correspond with the needs of its children, who each possess unique relational and learning patterns. Differences between individual pupils need not constitute a negative, but instead can be an educative and positive experience for mainstream teachers and pupils. All children need a school setting that provides the greatest growth potential for them.

Why is a mainstream classroom beneficial?

• The process of labelling and its ill effects are avoided.
• There is the possibility of upward mobility or educative progress in a mainstream setting if certain conditions are put in place to support the pupil.
• Much learning occurs between peers and beyond organized lessons.

Primarily, what is crucial is that every teacher takes responsibility for educating every child in their classroom. However, where necessary this must include access to other resources, such as specialist help in learning, language or behaviour. The teacher must understand the child's learning strategies and functioning and guide their education. If specialists are available they should be used to give advice, rather than remove responsibility from the teacher. The more human resources the teacher has to help to implement educational plans for the child, the better the pupil's learning situation will be in a mainstream setting. In accepting additional help the teacher is not removing herself from the centre of the relationship with the child, but allowing herself more intelligent involvement with colleagues and pupils.

All children are unique, and therefore different. For equity and justice in education to be realized, the overall quality of schooling must be investigated and improved, through the meeting of human differences in the ordinary or mainstream classroom.

The Salamanca Framework for Action (UNESCO 1994), the UN Convention on the Rights of the Child (1989) and the UN Standard Rules on the Equalization of Opportunities for Persons with Disabilities (1993) have created an international culture for inclusion by arguing that all forms of segregation are ethically unacceptable. Since the publication of the Warnock Report (DES 1978) in the UK, radical change has taken place in the strongly established institutionalized practices of educational categorization and segregation towards greater flexibility and acceptance of diversity in mainstream schools. They are as follows:

• The 1981 Education Act aimed at recognizing and meeting special educational needs within mainstream education.
• In 1986 the Education Act led to the creation of the National Curriculum, and required that the curriculum be differentiated for pupils of differing ability, experience and background.
• The Salamanca Statement (UNESCO 1994) called for the 'integration' of all pupils in mainstream classrooms.
• Two Green Papers, *Excellence for All* (DfEE 1997b) and *Meeting Special Educational Needs* (DfEE 1998a), were aimed at raising awareness of the way

that children with special educational needs were taught, with a particular focus on meeting their needs in local schools.

- The Integration Charter (CSIE 1989) argued for the need to integrate all pupils fully into ordinary schools. This was followed by the Inclusion Index (CSIE 2000), a means of enabling schools to check their inclusion practice against school indicators
- The revised Special Educational Needs Code of Practice, effective from January 2002, directs LEAs with detailed guidance to support, empower and challenge their schools to become more inclusive.
- The Special Educational Needs and Disability Act 2001 came into force on 1 September 2002 and makes it unlawful for schools and LEAs to discriminate against pupils with disabilities for reasons related to their disability without clear justification.

The 1981 Act established the principle that mainstream schools were to be responsible for organizing provision for children with SEN, who previously had been largely accommodated in special units or schools. Mainstream schools began to recognize that 'pupils with SEN were their responsibility' (Cowne 1998: 3). The 1988 Education Reform Act introduced the National Curriculum and the devolvement of funding to schools, which has had a significant impact on the acceptance, or otherwise, of pupils with SEN in mainstream schools. The Code of Practice on the Identification and Assessment of Special Educational Needs (1994) provided a practical framework as a consequence of the 1993 Education Act. This legislation laid the foundations for the development of the role of the school special educational needs coordinator (SENCO) as it is today, because it set out the principles for SEN in school and the key areas of responsibility of the SENCO. 'For the first time the nature and parameters of the SENCO's role and the procedures they had to follow were set out in some detail' (DfEE 1997b: 24). The government's Green Paper *Excellence for All Children: Meeting Special Educational Needs* (DfEE 1997b) further promoted inclusive practice and strengthened the subsequent Programme of Action (DfEE 1998b). National Standards for SENCOs were published in 1998. The revised Code of Practice emerged in 2000. It replaced the former notion of 'stages' to two 'thresholds' of school response to pupils observed to have different learning needs. The thresholds were designed to resolve the problem first through *School Action* and, second, through *School Action Plus*, using external agencies if necessary. It also revised and reasserted the role of the SENCO as a manager and coordinator of provision within the school.

The Disability Discrimination Act 1995 has been amended and replaced by the Special Educational Needs and Disability Act 2001. The Act strengthens the right of children with SEN to a mainstream education, and the support of parental choice for inclusive schooling. All aspects of school life should be reviewed to increase access to school premises and the curriculum. These are duties to be fulfilled through the new Code of Practice – not to be confused with the SEN Code. The Code, and a Code of Practice for providers of post-16 education with related services, has recently been made available to all schools via the Disability Rights Commission (DRC 2002).

These initiatives have been supported by numerous DfEE circulars. For example, Circular 10/99, *Social Inclusion: Pupil Support* (DFEE 1999), identifies groups at particular risk: pupils with special educational needs; children in the care of local authorities; minority ethnic children; Travellers; young carers; those from families under stress; and pregnant schoolgirls and teenage mothers. These initiatives are not solely aimed at pupils with SEN and enable the widening of access and support for many marginalized individuals and groups of children and young people in ordinary schools.

Many schools are involved in programmes that aim to accelerate the raising of educational standards in disadvantaged city or other urban areas by widening opportunities and intensifying support to pupils and their parents, often drawing on agencies and community interests to enhance this work. These initiatives include Education Action Zones, Excellence in Cities, the Single Regeneration Budget, the Ethnic Minority and Traveller Achievement Grant, the Standards Fund and the New Opportunities Fund. Many of these programmes focus on the achievements of targeted pupils and groups of pupils, including minority ethnic pupils, English as an additional language pupils who need particular support, gifted and talented pupils, pupils with special educational needs, children 'looked after' by the local authority and those children who are at risk of disaffection and exclusion. Special activities associated with such programmes might involve supporting the development of literacy, numeracy and information and communication technology (ICT) skills, study support, making alternative provision at Key Stage 4, improving continuity between the phases of education, encouraging greater parental involvement and family learning, and activities arising from the school's particular status as an early excellence centre, beacon or specialist school.

Among these initiatives are those attempting to include pupils who were formerly excluded from mainstream and special schools. Inclusive practices encouraged by these initiatives aim primarily at educating all children in their local communities. The communities that embrace inclusive education try to structure a school environment where the needs of every pupil are met and their aim is the successful education of all. All school staff, pupils and families work together to create supportive learning communities that ensure that each child learns to his or her potential and feels valued. Trying to establish inclusive education in a classroom or school involves adapting the curriculum and using a variety of teaching strategies to which pupils with diverse social, academic and learning needs respond. It has already been shown elsewhere that traditional mainstream curriculum and delivery approaches are frequently seen as irrelevant and uninteresting in relation to the diverse background and learning rates and styles of many pupils (Holt 1982; Smith 1986; Giangreco *et al*. 1994; Udvari and Thousand 1996; NASC 2001).

Never in recent history has there been so much government legislation and support for inclusive practice in mainstream. The changing attitude to inclusion is directly linked to changes in social and political thinking, influenced by a heightened awareness of equal opportunities, social justice, human rights and disability issues. This may be seen as a consequence of a 'constantly evolving public perception of what an education system should have as its priorities' (Oliver 1996). Alternatively, it may be seen as the government's means of cementing 'initiatives in education, social services and health, allied to powerful economic measures which aim to engage those who have become marginalised from Society' (Diamond 1995). This is not to deny, however, that there are many critics of inclusion (Reynolds 1995).

LEAs in the UK are developing procedures for inclusive practice, limiting the number of pupils in special schools and actively reducing the numbers of pupils with statements of SEN, at the same time offering 'value for money'. Yet there is evidence that some LEAs are unclear about what inclusion should mean in practice. Although generally they favour the development of more inclusive practice, they often interpret it as a 'state' rather than a 'process', and simply move pupils from special to mainstream provision without understanding its implications for the pupils involved (Ainscow *et al.* 1999).

Including pupils with special needs or other differences doesn't always require a radical disruption of existing school routines. Research has shown that teachers tend not to make radical changes to their existing teaching practices in response to having a pupil with a severe or profound intellectual learning disability in their classroom. Further, teachers become progressively more relaxed about inclusion and more supportive of it when they have had experience of it (Cowne 1998; O'Donoghue and Chalmers 2000).

A political change is taking place in schools, with mainstream and special schools working more closely together. The move to inclusive education means that mainstream schools are retaining or accepting new pupils who may have been segregated into special schools in previous decades. There is a greater emphasis on ways in which mainstream schools can widen access to, and participation in, the school life through curriculum support and the adoption of a more socially representative and wider pupil fellowship.

However, this shift in focus in mainstream education also takes place in a climate of 'exclusion'. Many pupils are still excluded from schools because of behaviour and alleged disturbance to classroom and school management. Although the number of permanent exclusions peaked in 1996/7, they have reduced since. Exclusions in 1996/7 were:

0.04 per cent of primary school pupils;
0.34 per cent of secondary school pupils;
0.64 per cent of special school pupils.

Permanent exclusions at present represent:

0.03 per cent of primary school pupils;
0.23 per cent of secondary school pupils;
0.36 per cent of special school pupils
(http://www.dfes.gov.uk/statistics/DB/SFR/s0275/tab001/html).

Children with special needs are six times more likely than others to be excluded, and 83 per cent of excluded pupils are boys. Pupils with statements of SEN (an estimated 0.3 per cent) are three times as likely to be excluded as pupils without statements (0.1 per cent) in 2000/1. Some groups are disproportionately affected, e.g. 16 per cent of permanently excluded children are of ethnic minority origin. The permanent exclusion rate among children in care is ten times higher than the average. Perhaps as many as 30 per cent of children in care are not attending any school, whether through exclusion or truancy. However, DfEE guidance states that exclusion should be used only in response to 'serious breaches of a school's policy on behaviour or of the criminal law' (DfEE 1997a).

With inclusive practice, all school parties have to adapt and adjust to make it successful. The emphasis now is upon a philosophy of acceptance of inevitable educational differences, based on making radical changes in the mainstream school to widen curriculum access. Diverse approaches to inclusion range from enabling all children with educational, social or cultural differences to be educated in local schools, to a more mixed range of provision. Each local authority in the UK interprets the inclusion ideal in its own specific manner to suit its political direction, geography, finances and existing traditional school provision. The DfES has funded many LEAs to increase effective inclusive practice in mainstream schools through annual funding and various initiatives, including sharing special school expertise, developing school networks to share and disseminate good practice and improving the quality of links between schools and parents (Richardson 2000; McCutcheon 2001). However, it is crucial to realize that, regardless of the rhetoric about inclusive practice, it is only when critical evaluation of various initiatives and projects is undertaken that they can be judged as being inclusive according to the values of the participants. For example, it is difficult to determine whether inclusive provision is successful without feedback from those involved in its practice, and evidence of a consensus of approval involving pupils and their parents.

Many LEAs have set up unified learning support services to provide the expertise necessary to support schools. Their purpose is to share expertise within the existing behavioural, learning, sensory and educational psychology teams in a multiprofessional manner. For example, Birmingham is establishing a network system to involve all community, community special, foundation, voluntary-aided and voluntary-controlled schools with support services in education, health and social services. It is hoped that these networks will give parents, carers and local community groups better access to more equitable services (Baldwin 2000). There are some localized examples of good practice in the UK, but overall progress towards inclusion is slow, often because of already existing and well established interests that exert power to retain the status quo. Government initiatives fund many LEAs to organize focused inclusion development work to supplement mainstream support arrangements already in operation.

In recent years schools have been forced to adopt changes to their policy and practice by outside influences, as a more equal and inclusive society is created. This move towards the greater inclusion of pupils with educational, cultural and learning differences comes at the same time as government direction to adopt more assertive disciplinary approaches within classrooms and to reduce pupil exclusion rates, as represented by legislation (DfE 1994; DfEE 1998b). The abolition of corporal punishment in schools represents significant social reform, yet it could be replaced by a more pervasive and intrusive pattern of vigilance and regulation. In every school there is a continuing problem of acceptable dress and behaviour, which may contradict the notion of schools operating as institutions committed to open access and retention of a more diverse pupil population. For example, the insistence on the wearing of school uniforms discriminates against groups such as Traveller families, who may be in the locality only for a short time. If inclusive practice is seen as a democratic negotiable process then the narrow interpretation of regulations needs to be mediated. The dynamic world of schools is marked by change and the continuing occurrence of unique situations, each of which can yield a variety of possible outcomes depending on the specific circumstances.

Peters (1966) claims that two aspects of education are badly in need of ethical foundations: its matter and its manner. Convincing evidence for the success of inclusive practice has to be analysed and publicized before it can be judged as ethical in every case. Arguments can be made that the end does justify the means, or does not always justify the means, or that the means–end distinction doesn't apply in this situation. Yet the assessment of ends and the choice of means to ends, and the imposition of values and standards on an ideal, cannot be used to justify 'any' educational changes, particularly in the current policy context, which translates values like 'inclusion' into targets and then refers to outcomes independently of pedagogy.

It is within this context that this book is written, as a means for teachers and educational professionals to deal with the practical and complex challenge of making inclusive practice a reality and to decide the extent of its ethical dimensions, because educational inclusion is also social inclusion. It involves the practice of equity and social justice in school practice and in curriculum adaptations. It means acknowledging and respecting everyone's right to contribute to, and network in, their local and wider communities.

This book aims to support schools, teachers, LEA advisors for ethnic minorities, SENCOs, their support staff, associated professionals and the associated community in the establishment of a capability to formulate a workable technology to support policy principles. The everyday school reality is riven with dilemmas and problems that serve to illuminate the complexities and inherent contradictions in working for inclusive educational practice. The advancement of teacher-led research, involving positive action in this area, entails taking risks, yet it is the only realistic way to solve practical problems arising from new educational initiatives such as inclusion. Teachers and other educational professionals using practitioner research will be enabled to investigate the complexities of the change process required for inclusive practice. It is hoped that they will be active protagonists in the promotion of investigatory and evaluative practice that brings about increased discussion and activity in schools to challenge existing constraints to the advancement of inclusive practice. This can be achieved in LEAs and schools by:

- the investigation of existing practice, and its evaluation as good practice for inclusion;
- the management of support mechanisms for the investigation, its development, dissemination and application;

- the involvement of pupils, parents, teachers, headteachers, psychologists and other educational professionals as co-participants in an inclusive and democratic research process;
- the organization of a stable support group to share evidence and information and to question or challenge the basis of the assumptions made by its participants.

CHAPTER TWO

Action research for inclusive practice

Action research improves practice by developing the practitioner's capacity for discrimination and judgement in particular, complex, human situations. It unifies enquiry, the improvement of performance and the development of persons in their professional role.

(Elliott 1991: 52)

Much has been written about how and where action research developed in the past century and into the new millennium. Yet its singular success has been in giving a greater voice to practitioners in the design and improvement of their own and their colleagues' work, and its development as a major mode of enquiry in professional development. It is increasingly being used in nursing, medical, social work and other institutional contexts as a form of professional evaluation and development.

This book is directed towards teachers and other professionals who wish to conduct research for purposes of improving their teaching or professional effectiveness, or of contributing to professional knowledge for social and educational inclusion. The emphasis is on an action research approach that includes reflective enquiry and practice and may help professionals as individuals, or in groups, to understand the nature of their assumptions, values and beliefs about policy and practice in their field. It provides the opportunity for professionals to review their practices, in their local contexts, for the purposes of change and improvement. Action research that focuses on pedagogical issues encourages teachers to become reflective practitioners. When practitioners become reflective, the processes of systematic and planned action can be integrated into personal and professional lives. For educational practice to become inclusive it must first become reflective.

What is being expanded in this book is an interpretive, discursive, democratic, inclusive and investigatory process using action research. Inclusive practice requires an investigation of its effectiveness, developed through a democratic discursive process that attempts to include all relevant participants in institutional contexts. The process aims to give its contributors and participants a voice in the investigation. It aims to ensure a democratic research procedure that demonstrates the above values, while at the same time defining and redefining them in the transactions integral to the investigation.

Action research was first created by the social psychologist Kurt Lewin (1946) while he was working for community action programmes in the USA in the 1940s. Interest in action research developed in Britain with the Ford Teaching Project, directed by Elliot and Adelman (1973). The practical focus of the British initiative led Australian academics to call for more 'critical' and 'emancipatory' action research (Carr and Kemmis 1986). There were similar developments in Europe (Brock-Utne 1980), and in subsequent decades action research became a worldwide means of supporting social and educational reform. Criticisms about its development are related to its becoming individualistic and dislocated from social action, the simplification of its strategies for pedagogic purposes, the use of language about action research and its potentially narrow conception of practice (McTaggart and Singh 1987). The use of the term 'practice' in action research needs clarification, and MacIntyre's early definition draws out the socially constructed, ideological nature of social practice as:

> any coherent and complex form of socially established co-operative activity through which goods internal to that activity are realised . . . with the result that human powers to achieve excellence, and human conceptions of the goods and ends involved, are systematically extended.
> (MacIntyre 1982: 175)

Practices are differentiated from the institutions in which they are developed. For example, a hospital or school is concerned with external goods, like survival rates or examination results, that are structured in terms of power and status: 'no practices can survive any length of time unsustained by institutions' (*ibid*.: 181). However, recent debate between Dunne and MacIntyre has caused some adaptation of this view:

> teachers are involved in a variety of practices and . . . teaching is an ingredient in every practice . . . All teaching is for the sake of something else and so teaching does not have its own goods . . . as with other practices, achieving the ends of teaching requires that teachers engage in the practice of making and sustaining the communal life of the school. So the communal life of the school is . . . a place of genuine, if small-scale, cultural achievement within which a variety of practices flourishes.
> (MacIntyre and Dunne 2002: 9)

The notion of teaching is extended to a variety of practices that sustain the community of the school, as well as meeting the school's technical ends, i.e. ensuring examination passes. The extension of that practice would include education as a practice. Teaching, it may be argued, is based on an overly narrow technical conception of practice. Schools are seen as institutions with a specific status and purpose where education for social inclusion may be practised. Teaching is taken to be a form of practice, a form of teaching for certain activities like music or literacy. Yet schools, because they are institutions, should be for educating pupils and not merely the technical task of transmitting knowledge and skills. One could therefore argue that teaching is not the only practice in schools, but education is.

Yet teaching is one's own practice of education, which includes its traditions, values and the internal and external goods necessary to its sustenance and progress. Action research is concerned with very wide forms of educational interaction, with traditions and internal values. It follows that action research for inclusive education critiques the values, processes and goods associated with the dominant educational tradition. Action research can take a broad, socially and politically aware perspective to improve inclusive practice through an investigation of teaching and learning. Inclusion requires educational investigation into its practices. It adopts an evaluative stance to teaching, its processes and outcomes, and reflects on the social and educational values that make inclusive practices successful.

Action research problematizes the values of the institution by challenging and questioning its practices in the institutional context, which can pose a threat to them. Therefore, action research needs to probe the moral foundations of the institution, while at the same time constructing local groups or communities that collaborate to sustain the moral and intellectual life of institutions. It is a risky and frustrating activity to try to raise awareness about moral responsibilities that have become obscured in the technical practices of institutions. To make inclusive practice a reality, moral aspects of institutional activities need to be addressed. Such challenges are best supported and achieved through discussion, debate and reflective action.

Action research for inclusion may be met with antagonism and hostility, because a collaborative commitment to explicit actions and practices will threaten institutional practices, especially those that rely heavily on bureaucratic procedures. Yet individuals who share similar values can theoretically be transformed into an action research group within an institution, by forming a self-reflective alliance or partnership that aims to question institutional activities and their authenticity in context. Such groups would take on the task of interpreting and reconstructing their world through an interactive dialogical process, since each member of a group takes their history and biography with them into the dialogue. Plans for change are based on dialogue, investigation and reflection, leading to deliberate action for educational and social improvement for better inclusive practices.

Small groups or critical communities may form in an organic sense, i.e. people with similar aims and values may view their institutional values and practices as problematic. Developing a form of critique together can be valuable in strengthening relationships and enabling people to work together for change. However, because such groups are organic, they are frequently working against hierarchical structures and defined role relations, and their collaborative existence may therefore be short. Yet because such groups create reflective space for the reconfiguration of the meanings of institutional action, they bond their members in a collaborative venture. They also allow dissent and resistance to be articulated in the context of reflective practice. Sharing similar concerns builds a feeling of collegiality among members, which supports their personal growth and gives them the freedom of expression and the space to investigate passionately held issues like inclusion. Regardless of how long an action research group stays together for a specific purpose, members learn about how such groups function and how, either individually or together, successes and failures related to its aims are perceived and understood.

So, to define action research, it is:

1 Overtly reconstructive, i.e. it questions and redefines the terms and conditions that shape practice.
2 Transformative, through personal and professional change in a democratic and inclusive investigatory process.
3 A form of self-discovery, self-development and self-understanding.
4 A potentially risky undertaking for the sake of a specific professional ideological value or aim, like inclusion.

Overtly reconstructive, i.e. it questions and redefines the terms and conditions that shape practice

Action research provides a means of raising awareness about inclusive educational practice at the local level to empower students, service receivers, stakeholders and professionals in social and educational contexts, thereby creating greater political and social awareness among educators, service providers and their clientele, children, young people, parents and pupils.

Action research has a political purpose that can propose an explicit political agenda, e.g. action for social justice, or against class, gender, ethnic, religious or race discrimination. In the investigation of situations with a specific focus on these issues, power and relationships are placed in the foreground. An evaluation of educational situations occurs, where politics, investigation and action are seen as one.

Action research involves colleagues and other participants in a shared activity, a process of change that might focus on the empowerment of oppressed groups and individuals within the social and educational systems of society. Action research is systematic practitioner enquiry, which can, if so directed, contribute to greater social, economic and political justice throughout the world. People who learn to become action researchers become part of the action research community, which enables them to use its techniques and the values they have learned in future professional contexts beyond the formal period of the research (James and Worrall 2000). The skills they learn in the process become a lifelong educational investment.

Educational research is often seen as a cynical enterprise if it is aimed simply at deeper understanding on a theoretical level. It is only when research reaches real human issues like inclusive practice and makes a real difference to human conditions that its support is strengthened. Action research may be predominantly directed towards specifics in the case under investigation, e.g. changing the delivery of the school curriculum in a particular school. This makes it very localized and context-bound, but nevertheless it can be effective through its local ownership of and responsibility for political action.

Although they may appear small and insignificant, every classroom issue has a political dimension. Political and critical issues are present in the everyday moral decision-making regarding the placement, assessment, teaching and care of pupils. The term 'practical science' is used to refer to a form of moral social discourse that involves teachers and other professionals in the generation and testing of practices that are ethically consistent with ideals and values associated with the research problems inherent in everyday routine, like the creation of inclusive practice (Elliott 1995a). Everyday choices in the practice of education reveal attitudes, values and moral commitments with regard to social inclusion and change. Whether we want to acknowledge it or not, we expose our deeply held values and convictions when these matters are discussed. Every classroom, social work visit or medical consultation is a site for the practice of greater educational equity and social justice. Other sites involve those who engage in the social, educational, economic, psychological and medical welfare of children and young people. Professional and teacher change is a necessary condition for systemic change, which in turn is necessary to bring about better inclusive educational practices.

Transformative, through personal and professional change in a democratic, inclusive, investigatory process

The successful lifelong development of professionals from a variety of disciplines provides a challenge to professional educators. The people who maintain the cultures of professional practice represent many different identities, experiences, understandings, capabilities and talents. Regardless of the means used to provide professional development opportunities for inclusive practice, or any teaching or learning endeavour involving adults, they inevitably attract participants from a wide range of backgrounds, ages and experience. This rich variety offers opportunities for collegial interaction and learning from others. The sharing of biographies deepens self-understanding, because the researcher's life history inevitably becomes part of the personal agenda for the inquiry in the action research process. No person who engages in a professional reflective inquiry can avoid personal involvement and development within a culturally transformative process. It is not sufficient to consider the use of the action research process itself as a means of successfully achieving planned action. There is no security in the mere intentionality of the inquirer's attempts to improve inclusive practice. The nature of the person and the situation becomes merely experimental, and may become trial-and-error, unless the persons involved recognize the personal, cultural, historical and often inherently prejudiced agendas that inform their situational perceptions and understandings. Without such recognition, there is also a danger of the researcher carrying out well intentioned but unethical research. For example, action may be taken at the expense of the pupil, e.g. the classroom is re-organized into 'sets' to improve the problem of noise, teacher control and group management. Yet this action may relegate pupils with particular social, cultural or learning differences into their own separated non-inclusive school work groups.

Action research acknowledges the presence and influence of subjective realities in the gathering and analysing of data. It is a form of practitioner development that affects institutional improvement and brings with it social change. This development is aimed at a higher quality of professional practice, e.g. for inclusive schooling to enable both teachers and pupils to develop the quality of their teaching and learning. Ideally, too, it is aimed at making society more democratic through the involvement of professionals from different disciplines, students, clients, service users, stakeholders, parents and children. This involvement aims to embrace all the research participants equally through a democratic investigatory process based upon the negoti-ation and exchange of information and ideas. Therefore, the action research process *for* inclusive practice is also action research *as* inclusive practice.

Democracy, when used in a broader political context, refers to a form of government in which the 'demos', the people, rule. Since its identification with political equality, its meaning has been extended to cover any applica-tion of the principle of equality. It is a term, like 'inclusion', that is inherently subject to definitional ambiguity, yet its practice provides the opportunity for minorities to take action and to voice their opinions and needs for societal changes. In an educational sense, Dewey (1966) claims that criteria for edu-cational criticism or construction, like inclusion, imply a particular social ideal. Two evaluative measures of its worth are the extent to which the inter-ests of a group are shared by all its members, and the fullness and freedom with which it interacts with other groups. 'A society which makes provision for participation in its good of all its members on equal terms and which secures flexible readjustment of its institutions through interaction of the different forms of associated life is in so far democratic' (Dewey 1966: 99).

The research process itself models democratic procedures that are fully inclusive and gives a voice to all research participants, especially to marginal-ized pupils, students and parents. Since democracy stands in principle for social continuity and free interchange, it implies a theory of knowledge by which one experience gives direction and meaning to another. Researchers may be striving to change traditional and received beliefs by emphasizing individual aspects of knowing. Yet knowledge is not a universal or fixed concept, so that transforming beliefs and long-held facts and values in pro-fessional practice leads to 'new' knowledge, which in turn can be challenged and transformed through democratic investigatory processes. This can be achieved by democratically formed and organized groups created for specific purposes like social justice and inclusion. The use of democratic and inclusive procedures is essential to the research process on three levels.

First, there is the voluntary inclusion of participants who understand what their role and rights are in relation to the research process and the final case record. Second, there is the researcher's and participant's co-sharing and feedback of information and ideas, which can occur with a friend or colleague or in a group. Third, all research participants are given an equal voice and equal opportunities to debate the issues that arise. All views are respected and included, regardless of their source and the status of their speakers. It is important that trust is created and maintained and that procedures for discourse are negotiated and agreed right from the start, when ideas are bounced off colleagues and feedback is given about research data and possible courses of action. The principal researcher is responsible for creating democratic, inclusive interaction and honest feedback to participants during the research process and in the research case record. The researcher is also responsible for ensuring, through a democratic, inclusive, discursive process, that evidence is discussed and planned action is validated by others before its implementation.

A form of self-discovery, self-development and self-understanding

In professional development for inclusive practice the everyday activities of the teacher researcher are open to scrutiny. The person's perception of himself or herself within the role becomes a topic for critique and reconstruction. Each professional practitioner has a view of what behaviour should be practised within the role, and exposing the reality to investigation by oneself and colleagues may be felt as threatening. It is important, therefore, that every researcher has some form of educational support for the investigation, to help to resolve its dilemmas and decide on challenges for action. Ideally, a form of organized group support enables the action research process, particularly if it is organized in a formative, constructive and democratic manner to allow its members to feel relatively safe to discuss their deeply held concerns as they relate to the emerging research data.

The process of changing a person within a role and the practical understanding of their actions rest upon the power and the politics of the change process to render the person or the educational group more effective in increasing inclusive practice (O'Hanlon 1995b). Yet often formal action research models do not appear to match adequately the reality of the experience, because of their impersonal and objective nature. Dadds found that:

> the teachers' descriptions and accounts of their work bore little resemblance to the tidiness of the [action] research models . . . Affective views of subjectivity were missing from reading but not from the teachers' experiences . . . I had a need for additional and different action research discourses.
>
> (Dadds 1995: 3)

A practitioner's subjective view and experience are the key to understanding the process of change, which notion is supported by Shulman's (1992) concept of pedagogical content knowledge based on experience. However, experience is educative only with reflection. The importance of the personal dimension of experience has been displayed in numerous teacher case studies (Nias 1980;

Clandinin 1986; Clandinin and Connelly 1986; Dadds 1995). Teachers acquire practical knowledge about what works best for inclusive practice by developing their personal narratives and biographies in interaction with the professional educational and teaching context. A number of research methodologies – such as narrative research and case studies – are common to all professional evidence-based enquiry, of which action research is a part. A group formed deliberately to discuss research evidence and its implications, using *interpretive discourse*, can enable such narratives to be created, discussed and recorded (see Chapter 4).

A potentially risky undertaking for the sake of a professional ideological value or aim, like inclusion

The validity of any abstract theory must lie in its practical potential (praxis, as defined by Aristotle 1955), *which is practice with ethically committed action that is morally informed.* It is practical activity and routine that is shaped by ideals and values, which are ends that cannot be realized independently of the direction they take in the situations they are played out in. Such ideals and values imply a specific form of practice, with an ethical dimension. The implementation of socially inclusive practice demands the evaluation of embedded values, attitudes and ideals. Inclusion practices are not simply the implementation of abstract accounts of what practice is recommended to be in imaginary situations. Inclusion practice based on a research process is a form of 'practical philosophy' with a focus in action. It is a research that creates knowledge about how to promote inclusive practice as an 'educational good' through ethically right action. Such knowledge can only point generally in the direction that actions for inclusive practice ought to take. It cannot predict the success of the practice in advance, because of the variety of influences implicit in different school and institutional contexts. It necessitates a form of reflection in which informed choice and judgement play a crucial role. It is a means of deciding not as much how something, like inclusion, is to be done as a rule, as what factors ought to be considered in different circumstances, by proceeding in a conscious and reflective manner, deciding between different means of achieving the same aim, or alternative means of reaching different aims. It is a way of resolving the many inevitable moral dilemmas that arise in the reconstruction of educational practices for inclusion. This involves taking risks in practice, trying out alternatives and allowing pupils to control their own learning when possible. It involves investigating taken-for-granted teaching practices and replacing them with strategies to support more equal practices and wider curriculum access.

Teachers consistently respond to the social and political implications of their practice through the process of action research. Often their investigations can be supported by postmodernist research methods, ideas and activities, where the world is viewed from a number of different and possibly incompatible points of view, providing an opportunity for personal challenge. Professional growth implies responding to such challenges. Teacher researchers have become adept at creating metanarratives, which expose the reality underlying superficial practices, through the process of critical reflection, multiple representations, language metaphor and discourse. For better inclusive practice it is important that risk-taking is an integral activity undertaken by all research participants, including children, young people and parents.

Teachers as researchers

It is teachers in the end who will change the world of education, by understanding it.

(Stenhouse 1983)

Adults approach a learning situation with some preconceived idea about what they are trying to learn, because they have existing knowledge based on a wide range of experiences. Making use of pre-existing knowledge demands an approach to professional and teacher education that values this knowledge. Teachers' experience and knowledge enable them to be reflexive. Dewey (1966) defines reflection as 'the reconstruction or reorganization of experience', which requires looking through one's mind to focus on a past experience. Reflection is a thorough inquiry (Dewey 1933; Schwab 1978) that questions the experience, so as to understand it better. Examination of past experience in a focused way leads one to learn and grow. Conversations and discussions with professionals and teachers about their past personal and professional experiences are a means of opening up their thoughts about influences on their beliefs and values and on their work and practice. Reflection encourages a deep, as opposed to a surface, approach to learning (Biggs and Telfer 1987; Entwhistle 1992).

Deep-level learning looks beyond basic assumptions about symbols and their meaning. It searches for relationships between ideas already held and those newly encountered. It encourages ownership of knowledge through self-reflection rather than reliance on an external authority. Reflective practice requires a commitment to learning from experience and from evidence, rather than a learning of certain prescriptions for action.

Simply to expect teachers to become reflective practitioners (Schon 1983) is to omit any detailed specification of how methodological competence as a reflective practitioner is to be developed. It is often assumed that reflection is a solitary and private process, facilitated by a mentor and aided by the keeping of a diary, journal or log. But this alone is inadequate to support the teacher in meeting the pressures associated with developing an inclusive school or an inclusive society.

Although the classroom is an important site for discursive action in the struggle for greater educational equity and social justice, research from other sources can provide additional evidence for the development of the action research. When outside collaborators contribute to the investigation, the terms 'insider' and 'outsider' are used to indicate different locational viewpoints, and a combination of evidence gathering from these two per-spectives may provide additional insights for reconstructive action research. In practitioner research it is the 'insider' who is exposing the research situation and taking action for change, with the insider's investigation revolving around himself or herself in a professionally challenging context. The collaborating 'outsider', however, takes fewer risks because he or she has much less professional investment in the process and is distanced from the outcomes of the research. The 'insider' may be struggling with bias, emotional involvement or coercion, whereas the 'outsider' operates from outside of the immediate realities and can therefore act as an anchor for wider discourse and interpretation, and diffuse situational tensions. It is possible that the 'outsider' can also become involved in 'insider' perspectives when gathering and interpreting evidence, yet an outsider perspective can more easily support and validate any problematic concerns. Externally produced knowledge can help us to gain a perspective on a situation or to link our efforts to the work of others (Rudduck 1985). However, Winter (1989) argues that 'insider' research is crucial, because wisdom derived entirely from the experience of others is 'at best impoverished and at worst illusory'.

The original reflective practitioner model of research created by Schon (1983, 1987) accepts researchers' mere intentions of possible active inter-vention. Action research goes beyond reflective practice by expecting planned actions to realize intentions, through intervention in situations deemed to be unsatisfactory. Planned action moves beyond mere aspiration to the active realization of deliberate practical improvements for inclusion.

Stenhouse (1983) believed that curriculum research and development ought to belong to the teacher, but this would require a change in their professional self-image and conditions of work to enable them to examine their own practice critically and systematically, structuring their understanding of their work. He advocated that teachers communicate with each other and report their work to accumulate case studies similar to those in medicine. He believed that fruitful development in the field of curriculum and research depended upon evolving styles of cooperative research by teachers.

Action research is collaborative. It can use professional researchers like academics to contribute, direct, advise and evaluate. It involves a wide range of educational stakeholders, e.g. pupils, parents and administrators. It becomes an inclusive process when the research participants are fully representative of the research focus; for example, research into 'disaffection' includes con-tributions and comments from pupils and parents, as well as teachers and other professionals. Action research is a means of gathering and analysing information in order to change or improve educational practice in schools or other educational organizations and institutions. Teachers and other pro-fessionals grapple daily with problematic issues in their schools and organiza-tions, and are searching for help to develop skills to improve their practice. Professional development and training often focus on topical educational innovations that do not meet the needs of teachers and other educational professionals in the long term. They also propose a 'deficit' rather than a 'human potential' model of education (Rogers and Kutnick 1990). Through action research, teacher researchers learn to develop skills that enhance their understanding of school and classroom complexity, providing a deeper understanding of their everyday decision-making related to inclusive practice. What is involved is not as much doing something that others suggest, as it is a conviction that action should be taken, based on research evidence and reflection, supported by collegial interpretive discourse about possible actions.

An implicit principle in action research is the reflection on and monitoring of the professional's judgement in action. Schon (1987) points to the distinction between reflection *in* action and reflection *on* action. He describes reflection in the midst of action, a kind of reflection in present professional activities that may change our actions. He writes: 'Our thinking serves to reshape what we are doing while we are doing it . . . in cases like this . . . we reflect *in* action.' However, reflection that has no direct connection to present action, that takes place retrospectively after the events, is reflection *on* action. Schon writes: 'We may reflect *on* action, thinking back on what we have done in order to discover how knowing in action may have contributed to an unexpected outcome.' Professional improvement rests on the intentionality of the action, and the deliberate planning and development of action, which may be monitored in the practice. Yet it can only be properly interpreted and understood in the reflection *on* action, or in the planning for action that evolves from it.

The teacher researcher is engaged in practical reasoning in day-to-day attempts to improve the inclusiveness of his or her situation. It is only when we take stock of the activities and practices later that we have the opportunity to evaluate the complexities of the situation. This reflection on action may occur when the person is alone, deliberating on the data, e.g. writing a journal or log, listening to an audio recording, reading observation notes. It may occur in discussion of the evidence with a group of colleagues or participants, or with a friend or tutor. The reflection *in* action becomes secondary to the reflection *on* action because of the immediacy of the demands of practice, which requires that the professional acts immediately, and makes quick judgements about taking action, which, when they are later recalled, may become distorted. Anecdotal records are not factual records. They are an interpretation, through recall, of what has actually happened.

The research evidence that results from the monitoring and recording of practice 'as it happens' reveals aspects of the practice that are often hidden or masked through reflection *in* practice. The complexity of the social action, as it occurs, often prevents productive reflection from happening *in situ*. There are also multiple relationships between experience and language. The relationships allow one to explore and play in conversation and discussion, depending on who the listeners are. What has taken place is transformed through its interpretation when past events are talked about. A deeper awareness and understanding develops when one reflects *on* action. There are some things, however, that one's memory may deliberately suppress. Emotional states are not always consciously realized when one is dealing with immediate professional concerns. The professional may be incapable of acting other than he or she does because of established learned reactions, and may not realize how personal emotional overlays are affecting the situation and might need to be controlled. One's emotional state can be recalled when reflecting on action, and thus feelings and emotions will also be amenable to transformation in plans for future action. The transformational opportunity for professionals resides in their potential to reflect *on* action.

Knowledge is constructed by a person in interaction with the environment, resulting in both environmental and individual change as a consequence of the learning process. In this constructivist view of learning, knowledge cannot be separated from action: they work together in a dialogical manner. It is in the social interaction that cultural meanings are shared and then become 'owned' by individuals. Therefore, teacher researchers who investigate their own institutional and constructed environments are changing themselves and their surroundings in the process of constructing knowledge. Knowledge is not theoretical in the sense of consisting of a state of mind that is detached from action in the world. For teachers, it is learning that occurs in interaction with the school and the classroom, where professional knowledge is transformed and recreated (Elbaz 1983; Schon 1983; Fenstermacher 1986; Calderhead 1988; Elliott 2000b). A parallel to the growth of knowledge through action occurs in the development of interpersonal skills, including negotiation skills and personal confidence in expressing views and intentions. This development involves the practitioner's cognition and emotion, combined with a commitment to specific ideals, such as inclusive schooling. It is the whole person communicating in everyday professional and institutional activities, combining the personal and professional roles, who works for improved practice for inclusion. There is general agreement that action research has been a major experience in teachers' personal and professional development and has also been transformative in their practical working lives (Day 1984; Grundy and Kemmis 1988; Webb 1990; Elliott 1998; Ainscow 1999). Pring supports such a view with his assertion that 'The notion of teacher as researcher is important . . . it is a reassertion of the crucial place of professional judgement in an understanding of a professional activity' (Pring 2000: 138).

In conclusion, teachers learn about their teaching through an active process in which they construct knowledge and understanding from experiences provided by themselves and others. They do so in ways that are shaped by their personal characteristics, individuality and previous learning. Teaching is a responsive activity that requires the development of skills which are heavily dependent on the context where the learning occurs. With experience in many different classroom situations, teachers may develop a repertoire of technical skills to use in a particular classroom situation to improve inclusive practice. This implies that teaching, which is built upon learning, requires both ethical and technical competence to be continually developed through a process of investigation and self-evaluation. This is inherently an action research process. In time, teachers can choose for themselves which professional development opportunities best suit their needs. They can learn new skills for inclusive practice that can be sculpted to 'fit' their professional character, experience and expertise within the wider school culture.

In summary, then, action research supports inclusive practice by:

- using research evidence as the rationale for change and deliberate action to improve unsatisfactory situations;
- planning active intervention for inclusion through participant evaluation and active feedback;
- encouraging personal growth and freedom of expression with participants in the research process;
- providing opportunities for change through democratic interpretive discourse and inclusive investigation;
- building collegiality and partnership with like-minded people;
- improving the quality of educational and social practice for inclusion.

What are the criteria for good action research?

How can the quality of the process be gauged? Are there criteria that can be used to validate the action research process? Criteria for the validity of action research have been created by many groups for teaching and assessment purposes, and at international conferences. An all-embracing list of criteria created by one group of conference participants is as follows:

- credibility, established by the voice of the researcher being made public;
- inclusion of the researchers' values, beliefs and assumptions;
- clarity of the research question or issue, the purpose of the research and its process;
- incorporation of revisions in the direction of the research and changes in practice resulting from it;
- assurance that practical action strives to achieve educational aims;
- explicit connections made between the research and the learners to whom the educational aims are directed;
- demonstration of a self-critical stance towards practice and research;
- bringing multiple perspectives to the data and ensuring accuracy in its handling through self checking;
- addressing an issue that is of interest to others in the educational community;
- presentation of sufficient and convincing evidence to support assertions and claims made in research reports or in practice;
- conclusions following directly from the evidence;
- transferability to other situations, i.e. something similar could be done by others;
- inclusion of new questions and insights that arise from the research;
- characterization of the work as unfinished, a continuing venture;
- provocation through the setting of challenges to others and oneself in the ideas presented;
- demonstration of the importance of the research as the justification for doing it (Tickle 1995).

The predominant criteria for the assessment of action research refer to making it public, with a transparent practitioner researcher value position. The technical aspects of action research are related to clarifying the research focus, ensuring its valid evidential basis, taking action for the benefit of learners and meeting the wider needs of the educational community. What is traditionally excluded from the quality of the action research process is further advanced in this book. It is related to democratic and inclusive research procedures, the modelling of inclusive practice through the research process and the use of friends, colleagues or a research group to clarify and verify the evidential basis for action via interpretive discourse.

Elliott (1995a) defines the criteria for good action research as:

- aiming to realize professional values;
- integrating practice and research;
- developing the curriculum;
- implying reflexive practice and not simply reflective practice;
- involving the gathering of data about practice from different points of view;
- defining rather than applying quality indicators.

The emphasis is on developing professional ideals, changing practice, problematizing assumptions and beliefs, testing out new forms of action and professional practice as a form of research in itself.

The intention of this book is to influence readers to act inclusively when researching, by involving the research participants in conversations in which they have an interest or stake, except where verbal exclusion is justified, for example, by lack of language or communication skills. Inclusion is locationally specific and its discourse includes many different groups. Inclusion is more than an academic question; it encourages a plurality of views that require action in the real world. Conversations within an inclusive community evaluate activities according to standards that are acknowledged to be non-absolute and located, and that needs to be seen as fallible and subject to revision by the members of its communities.

CHAPTER THREE

Getting started: the research focus and issue; finding the petrific mace

Any significant problem involves conditions that for the moment contradict each other. Solution comes only by getting away from the meaning of terms that is already fixed upon and coming to see the conditions from another point of view, and hence in a fresh light. But this reconstruction means travail of thought.

(Dewey 1990: 181)

Getting started

You can begin by thinking about a *problematic situation* that needs to be addressed. The research questions are then investigated and action is taken for their amelioration. Any situation raises certain questions, which in turn can create research *questions*, e.g. how can learning support assistants (LSAs) help with inclusive practice in the school? Or is the school making full use of LSAs to improve the support of pupil learning in the classroom? You may also choose to start with an *issue*, e.g. some staff feel that LSAs should take over the teacher's role when administrative tasks are pressing.

The problematic situation is generally heartfelt and pressing. The situation is causing concern, like a feeling that the school or you, in your classroom, are not making full use of the LSA. The research *questions* are straightforward queries that can be explored through investigation. An *issue* is usually a contentious action or statement about an aspect of practice that is questionable or controversial. The general research *topic* in each case might be similar, as in the above examples regarding the support role of the LSA.

The research methods are planned in relation to the research topic, questions and issues. It is important to focus down on the questions and issues specific to inclusion in the context of the topic to be investigated. What is involved is a process of continual problem-solving, which may raise more questions than answers. The topic and specific focus will vary from school to school, teacher to teacher etc., but, universally, the areas for action will inevitably encompass:

- changes to the school culture and climate to make schools a more inclusive working environment for teaching and learning;
- the development of collaborative working relationships among and between teachers, SENCOs, non-teaching staff, pupils and outside agencies;
- structural and organizational change (timetabling etc.), to include co-operative arrangements with external services and other schools;
- the use of technologies to increase the effectiveness and efficiency of teaching, learning and assessment;
- improvement of the learning of all pupils, with due regard to differences in ability, social background, race and language.

Table 3.1 uses examples of inclusion topics that might form a basis for developing a rationale for change. It provides an illustration of the wide

Table 3.1   Topics for developing a rationale for change

Teaching and learning
Encouraging teacher collaboration in schools.
Maintaining learning standards, assessment and outcomes.
Ensuring pupil differentiation.
Monitoring inclusion in the National Curriculum.
Encouraging pupil interaction and developing communication.
Modifying and adapting resources, books, IT sources etc. for individuals and
    groups.
Enhancing instructional activities for individual or pupil groups.
Ensuring choice of subjects and an adequate and appropriate range of teaching
    methods.

Resourcing (personnel and technical support)
Providing new technology for all pupils.
Funding of support and technological personnel.
Funding for specific technical needs of pupils with differences.

Legislation and institutional policy
Making national and school policy that includes all pupils.
Devising school networks for inclusion.
Ensuring policy and practice are fair and just.
Ensuring policies are practised once created.

Gender, ethnicity, culture and race
Creating enabling environments for all pupils.
Creating awareness and understanding of diverse human needs in schools.
Creating cultural awareness of specific social, cultural and ethnic groups.

Family collaboration and support
Finding out about the experiences of families.
Building a sense of community.

Para/professional support
Judging the need for school therapists, support assistants, language assistants
    etc.
Ensuring schools have information about pupils' medical, religious and cultural
    differences.
Encouraging parent, school and peer communication and support.

Management and organization
Organizing a student-centred approach.
Organizing school-wide approaches to support different learning needs.
Ensuring services are based on pupil need rather than location.
Organizing effective resource and collegial management for inclusion.
Deciding on location and use of school buildings.

Integration of services
Integrating service support in the local area.
Integrating services for the under-fives.

Assessment and school placement
Identifying pupils' different educational needs.
Making decisions about pupils' school placement.
Identifying and assessing pupils with learning differences.

Access issues
Making decisions about access to mainstream schools.
Ensuring equal opportunities concerning the curriculum and wider school
    agenda.

Oppression and prejudice
Recognizing attitudes and values and understanding how they work.
Recognizing personal agendas and threats to pupil identity.
Reconciling contradictory values in the professional context for social inclusion.

Equality of treatment
Establishing a democratic school ethos for equality and justice in practice.
Recognizing and valuing different individuals and groups.

Education for choice and empowerment
Opening up new opportunities for pupils.
Enhancing pupil self-esteem.
Listening to pupils and finding out what they need.
Developing self-advocacy in and outside the school.
Preparing pupils for independence and independent living.
Learning about citizenship and democracy.
Developing a critical research agenda for the evaluation of professional practice.

range of possible topics that can form possible research questions and issues associated with inclusive practice. Table 3.1 can be used as a checklist for getting started and for finding a research focus. Discussion with colleagues will ensure that the research question is relevant to you and will contribute in some way to whole-school development. There is a need for the practitioner researcher to contextualize their specific situational problems and to develop ownership of the investigation. Careful consideration needs to be given to what is possible in any situation; therefore, Table 3.1 serves only to demonstrate the wide range of topics possible in the investigation of inclusive practice.

Another means to reflect on possible foci for research is provided by the Index for Inclusion (CSIE 1989), which is a valuable resource for finding a research topic with a particular meaning for specific situations. The Index offers a means of self-evaluation of school policy and practice. Schools may use the Index in whatever way suits them, or as an initial support for reviewing glaring omissions in school cultures, policies or practice.

It is also possible to build up your own alternative research questions based on current pressing situations giving cause for concern. An action research approach offers positive benefits to schools that are reflective and evaluative, and aim to become more inclusive. Its value lies in its use as a resource for changing practice. There is a danger that too many issues will be raised that would then need to be prioritized with colleagues. If a school decides, for example, simply to concentrate its efforts on aspects of classroom teaching, it may be an opportunity missed for wider social school change. But if action research is allowed to develop, with enough time for investigation and reflection through collaboration and collegial support, small classroom concerns may develop into school-wide issues for change, as, for example, with Meg (see case study below).

To begin, it is important to ask yourself why a particular question or issue matters to you. Reflect on your professional history and how your values and interests influence your choice of research topic. Write a short autobiographical introduction to the research, reflecting on your educational values and whether they are emulated through your practice, your school or nationally. Ask yourself, 'Why is inclusion important for me, why am I interested in its practice and is it in my interests to practise it? Is there a divergence between the ideal and the real view of inclusion in my educational world?'

This establishes where you stand in relation to your choice of research topic and the possible bias you may carry with you into the investigation. The autobiographical account can act as a guide when one is confronted with contradictions in the way evidence is collected and interpreted. It can also provide explanations for ambiguities in practice when one is critically challenged by friends or colleagues. A key factor in the deliberations is the value position of the researcher, the people in the situation and the educational culture.

The development of inclusive practice demands collegial support; therefore, negotiation with colleagues is a necessary condition for success. There may be school development priorities or vested interests to consider. There may be a lack of clarity about roles and responsibilities related to the LSA. There may be sensitivities about the school's success record with specific pupils, e.g. ethnic minority or Traveller pupils.

Unlike many other research methodologies, action research is not amenable to the design of a static research plan. When a research plan is being compiled, it is the process and direction of the research, rather than its outcomes, that are crucial. The plan should include the initial research question or issue, followed by initial speculation in response to the following questions:

1 What do I (we) want to uncover in the research?
2 Will the research lead to better policy or practice for inclusion?
3 What types of evidence are needed to answer the research question?
4 What can be learned from other relevant research on inclusive practice?
5 How will the evidence be collected, with and from whom?
6 How will the data be interpreted?
7 How will the evidence be recorded for the purpose of reflection and interpretation?
8 Has time been built in to discuss the evidence and allow ongoing feedback from participants?
9 How will records of evidence be compiled to justify the interpretations and conclusions reached?
10 How will the process of gathering evidence, its analysis and dissemination be organized to fit time schedules for the research?
11 Are there any financial implications of the research that need to be supported?

For example, you may, with the hypothetical question 'How do LSAs support inclusive practice in the school?', begin with some answers to these questions as follows:

1 We want to find out what exactly LSAs do in the classroom.
2 We hope the research will give us information about their practice that we can interpret with respect to updating the school inclusion policy and influencing school-wide practice.
3 The evidence we will need is detailed observations of LSAs in the classroom, their attention to individual or groups of pupils, time spent with pupils, time spent with the teacher, time spent in preparation and clearing up, and the organization of lesson plans and tasks with the teacher. Further, what form the lesson follow-up with the teacher takes, and how unexpected problems are resolved in the classroom when possible disruption occurs. Other research questions will arise from issues identified after the initial data collection, to check on what is actually happening in the classroom.
4 We will trawl the literature related to the use of LSAs in books, journals and through information technology. We will talk to colleagues and others about their use of LSAs.
5 The evidence will be collected via observational checklists devised after

initial observations have been carried out. LSAs will be interviewed. They will be invited to triangulate the data with the class teacher, colleagues and pupils. Other teachers, pupils and those associated with the issues that emerge will be involved in individual and group discussions. If any audio or video evidence is seen to throw light on difficult data, then this will also be employed in consultation with participants.

6 Interpretation of the data will take place within a coding frame, agreed in relation to data emerging from interview transcriptions, questionnaires and so on *in situ*. Frequencies and percentages will be tabulated, if appropriate, from observational checklists. Data will be presented in bar charts and tables as appropriate. However, it is expected that most of the data will be qualitative, and will be combed for relevant categories, keywords and phrases that tell us something we need to know. Expected information will be contrasted with unexpected information and charts of the data will be drawn up under appropriate research subheadings. The meaning of the data will be the yardstick for selection for the research record. Selection of data and their significance will be justified throughout.

7 We will keep a research log of all the data, which will be under the control of one person. Data from the log will be shared at staff meetings and with a research group beyond the school. Staff and colleagues in both groups will be invited to keep a research journal and to share their views at joint meetings.

8 We need to consider how time can be carved out to ensure ample discussion of what is taking place as the research develops. If it can be agreed, time could be taken during breaks or after the official school closing; otherwise, we will need specially designated time for the research.

9 Agreement must be reached about the official account of the research. Continual discussion and feedback during the data collection and interpretation will take place. Triangulation of data is essential to widen perspectives and any serious disagreements will be arbitrated by a neutral 'outsider'. If the final research record does not have consensual agreement then disagreements will be noted to the satisfaction of the participants.

10 Deadlines can only be negotiated during the research process. The time for the beginning and the end of the research can be decided in advance, but in the interim, other deadlines and meetings will need to be negotiated *in situ*.

11 There may be financial implications of finding time outside of the working day, i.e. the cost of cover for staff when meeting or collecting data. There may also be financial considerations related to the collection of data via observation, and other instruments, e.g. cost of audio or video equipment and tapes. There may be a need to pay for the transcription of tapes and the time spent on interpretation of data.

No one proceeds with a practitioner research project on their own. Everyone needs support and feedback from others in the initial choice of research topic and the subsequent planning of action from the implications of the evidence collected. If you are part of a research support group then colleagues in the group can act as advisors and critics and help to guide your plans for change. Simply taking action as a result of interpreting evidence on an individual basis is a risky endeavour. Everyone needs to reflect on the evidence, consider possible alternative interpretations of the data and, through discussion with others, decide on what is the best course of action for proceeding. The initial evidence, to confirm that the research question is a worthwhile and genuine basis for investigation, is critical to the direction of the research. Often, right from the start, one's perception of the situation can be mistaken, which comes to light in the collection of data. Therefore, the right focus for individuals in specific professional situations is crucial to success.

When the research question or issue is confirmed as a genuine one through the initial data collection, proceeding from the implications of the evidence is a matter of deciding what the priority is for further investigation. Many possibilities might suggest themselves, but only one research avenue should be developed through consultation and discussion with others, to deepen understanding of the original research issue. When exceptional circumstances arise it may be necessary to adapt to the changing situation, which requires a temporary change of focus before reverting back to the initial research topic. This can be illustrated by a case study of a teacher with whom I worked.

Meg, a primary school teacher, was keen to develop better inclusive practice in her school. Her story illustrates how a micro research issue can become much more, and grow to a whole-school issue through action research. Beginning with an initial small-scale research concern can, with flexibility and understanding, lead to major school change.

Meg applied for an action research based university postgraduate course, because she was very concerned about some pupils in her class with disruptive behaviour who were causing her management problems. She felt they were not getting 'the best' from her teaching. The pupils were not designated as 'special educational needs' pupils but were defined as 'in need of additional support in reading'. Because I was acting as her supervisor for the action research project, I could not find out directly the extent of the problem she explained. Therefore, I asked her, 'How can we investigate this concern and find if it is a worthwhile research issue to investigate?'

Meg said, 'Well, I've got so many problem pupils in my classroom. I have at least five pupils in my classroom who constantly disrupt my teaching and the other children's learning. I must do something about it, which is the reason that this is going to be the focus of my action research project.' Her research question was: how can I manage the behaviour of pupils who behave disruptively in my classroom?

I replied, 'Tell me the kinds of behaviour that you find disruptive and exactly what the pupils are doing.' She began by identifying the pupil behaviours. 'They run around the classroom, they are constantly going to the toilet, interfering with other pupils' pens, pencils and books. It's just chaos', she said. I proposed that we write down all these behaviours in a logbook, and then check that they were occurring against the names of the pupils, i.e. the 'five' causing problems. In this way, we could validate that the situation was actually occurring as she believed it was, and then proceed to find some constructive action to improve the situation. We needed evidence that the initial situation was as she described it before proceeding, on the grounds that one's beliefs and perceptions are not always consonant with the reality. I said, 'Now we have identified the pupils' behaviours we can make a checklist and then observe and check them in the classroom. Perhaps you can take some photographs too, using the checklist and your own note-taking of any incidents or behaviour you find particularly disturbing in your lessons. Come back next week and we will review the evidence together and decide how best to progress.'

She returned the following week looking disappointed. 'Well, how did you get on?' I asked. She replied quietly, 'You know, I don't have as much in the logbook as I thought I would have. I thought it would be full of ticks against the five children, especially John – he is the worst of the lot, but he only went to the toilet twice during lessons this week. There is really only one pupil who is much more disruptive than the rest, but things aren't too bad really when I look at the evidence.' I then said, 'Maybe we need to look at what is happening in the classroom in more detail. Have you thought about the time when unsettled behaviour occurs and what is happening in the classroom at the same time?' She agreed that she needed more evidence before we could proceed to define the exact issue for investigation. For the next week she added time and duration to the checklist of pupils' behaviour.

She returned for the next supervision looking very happy and said, 'It is so obvious. I didn't realize before that these problems are occurring, because they are the "reading support" pupils, the pupils with reading difficulties. We have a reading support teacher who comes into the school daily and she calls these same five pupils out every morning to go with her to her room for extra help with reading. I have found, by keeping the time check when the disturbing behaviour occurs, that it is just before and after they come back from their reading support lessons that these pupils are disrupting the classroom. It's so obvious!' I said, 'Yes, it is obvious. Perhaps they don't really feel connected to your classroom work. Are they being disrupted by removal to another room for reading support?' She replied, 'Yes, it's so obvious. I think I will have to talk to the reading support teacher, perhaps we can find a solution to the problem. We can then try to find a strategy to help them which is less disruptive to my classroom and to them.'

In time, after many discussions and further collection of evidence in her classroom, Meg encouraged the reading support teacher to come into her classroom. Sue, the reading support teacher, integrated the pupil's reading activities into the learning activities prepared for other pupils in Meg's classroom. Sue was pleased to offer help to a small group of pupils in the mainstream classroom and found that no time was wasted, as previously happened when pupils were moved from one room to another. Moreover, the pupils concentrated well on the reading tasks in hand, which were more closely related to Meg's lesson. It was a successful change. The five pupils settled down and caused few problems, as was evident from a continuation of Meg's observation and note-taking in her logbook. She also asked pupils themselves where they preferred to have their reading support and why. She monitored their achievements in literacy, which increased visibly in a number of months. Meg herself became very self-confident through her ability to resolve this issue, and wanted to progress further with it.

She then said, 'I wonder what's happening in the rest of the school. If I think of it as only my problem it isn't realistic. The problem may be magnified ten times in the ten other classrooms in my school. I will talk to the other teachers about it and find out.' She talked to the other teachers about her research and the changes it made to her teaching and the pupils' learning. She interviewed the staff individually, and questioned them, again to confirm that her hypothesis about their sharing her original research question was correct. She decided that something had to be done about similar problems in other classrooms in the school. She approached the headteacher and the governors with her research findings. She collected all the evidence she needed to convince them of a plan that was similar to changes she had made in her classroom. She photographed her lessons and collected evidence from other teachers in the school, who were observing their pupils and talking to them about their preferred learning locations. She convinced everyone of the value of the plan to use the reading support teacher in the mainstream classroom, rather than withdrawing pupils from lessons. Pupils had confirmed that they didn't like withdrawal, because they felt excluded from what was taking place with their friends and peers who remained behind. After a number of staff meetings that Meg initiated, and the sharing of evidence from lessons throughout the school, the headteacher, governors and staff agreed with her that they would make school-wide changes. They began to transform the school and to change the support teaching in every classroom as a direct result of her findings. There was a replication of her initial issue throughout the school, but no one had realized that other teachers shared the same school-wide problem.

Meg began her research as just one individual teacher with a small classroom problem. She then developed into someone who transformed not only the organization of her own classroom but also that of the entire school. From a micro issue, a major school change took place, with Meg as the central agent. She was able to lead the way because she became empowered by her investigative learning, which increased her self-confidence. Her planned changes were built upon finding evidence to support arguments for renewed action, through collaboration and discussion with colleagues, through the sharing of evidence with her collegial group at the university and through the involvement of pupils in their own choice of learning location.

This account of a teacher's action research clearly demonstrates a number of factors related to finding a problematic situation in action research:

- the strategic importance of beginning with a research question that is viable and workable;
- finding an issue that is compelling and felt, rather than artificial and contrived;
- involving colleagues, pupils and the whole school in the investigation of shared issues.

Meg was concerned about the inherent individual restlessness of some pupils and saw her main classroom question as being about engaging and including all pupils in classroom activities. Classroom observation allowed her to confirm which pupils were restless and when, and whether other pupils were also behaving in the same manner at the same time, indicating a wider classroom management issue for investigation. A colleague helped to observe in the classroom, providing useful feedback and triangulation of the data.

Data collection: analysis or interpretation?

We may feel constrained by the methods traditionally used to collect data, such as questionnaires and interviews. Creating new methods and experimenting in how to get the information we want will inevitably lead us into new research techniques. For example, it is now accepted that research journals and autobiographical and biographical stories are now valid evidential sources, whereas in decades past they were treated with great caution for higher degree work in educational institutions. Data is evidence and can be collected in everyday practice with technological instruments or with the help of preorganized questions, checklists and written records of what is happening. The data when collected must be recorded, i.e. made into a record for someone else to access. Once the data is recorded it can be interpreted or analysed. I prefer to use the term 'interpretation'. Most qualitative data, and the data gathered by teacher researchers, is interpreted, not analysed, because there are no steadfast or scientific means of analysing the data. It depends upon what the data means to different people, because it is filtered through our own sensibilities and theoretical perspectives. From the primary data – the data collected first hand by you or your colleagues – the teacher researcher moves to a research log or journal comprised of notes and preliminary interpretations based on this data. The move from primary data may involve coded notes and memos that have been made to make sense of the data. It is at this stage that the researcher attempts to give the data meaning and form through tables, charts, keywords, themes or phrases. Data is segmented into meaningful units and categorized according to an organizing system that derives from the data itself. Data is compared by the identification of likeness and differences. It is also about being surprised. If something comes as a surprise to you, that is significant, because it is unexpected. Categorization at this stage is tentative and preliminary, because it must remain flexible for possible modification later (Tesch 1990). The teacher-researcher may need to go over and over the data again in what feels like a cyclical process. A first draft of the data interpretation may be given to a friend or colleague for feedback, although it can be expected that a continual process of revision through feedback and discussion will lead to a public research record. The problem we face in data gathering is not to collect the data, but to select from it, interpret it and get rid of what we don't need. There will always be more data than you need, and continuous collection of data may be useless, because it only repeats what you have already found. It is combing of the data that helps us to edit it and decide what is unimportant to the research. We must decide what the story is that we want to tell. We only want to communicate the essence of the research story, with some process details, such as journal records, problems or constraints. We do not want to report everything simply because we have collected data that may be wasted.

There will come a time in this interpretation when decisions will be made about how literature and other sources of information led to understanding. An interpretation of theoretical perspectives will inevitably need to include personal theorizing, together with attitudes, values and opinions. The resulting record might point towards the development of new ways of understanding and theorizing. A key point in data analysis is to focus on *how* sense is made of the evidence, as well as *what* sense is made of it.

Remember that data collection can also be handled by pupils in school contexts. They can become useful allies and participants in research when they are instructed to act as observers, recorders, photographers, video photographers and editors of their own evidence, such as tapes, films and notes.

Using the literature

The choice of literature is related to the development of a rationale for the research methods, the pros and cons of selecting specific data-gathering and research procedures in different contexts, and the existing literature relevant to the research topic. The use of information technology, libraries and discussion with tutors, friends and colleagues is valuable. Academic and professional journals, newspapers, magazines and bulletins, and the media generally – i.e. television, radio and video – are all important means of informing the research arguments. Literature should be used not as a superficial means of supporting arguments, but more to stimulate, challenge and open up new thinking on the subject. The validity of the literature sources can only be judged in conjunction with their purposes. In action research, which is an exploratory methodology, the literature is sought when the research issues emerge from the evidence. This is different from the position in other forms of research, which require a search of the literature from the start, this influencing the direction of the investigation and its arguments. Literature helps to illuminate the research issues pursued and to bring micro research issues into a wider educational network. The literature can be from any sources seen to be appropriate, if supported by a claim for its authentic use. Green (1999) claims that she found that casual conversations with friends and colleagues put her in contact with interesting literature and ideas, outside her own field in action research. The real resources for learning rarely come from traditional ways of finding them.

Deconstruction

Deconstruction originated in literary criticism as a means of analysing texts (Derrida 1978). Deconstruction is difficult because it forces one to challenge the ideology of the predominant culture one inhabits. Most of us act from our ideological positions, i.e. from an unreflective certainty about practices like inclusion. We need reflective space to focus on gaps in the culture, to perceive how our claims are often saying something that can be challenged and contradicted. We can often see these contradictions in the data and its interpretation, especially in relation to inclusive practice. When we dig deeper we find more complexity. For example, everyone knows how subtle the writing of a job reference for a colleague can become, because of what is *not* said rather than what *is*. Interpreting and reading a reference requires one to consider what is not said, what is omitted and deliberately avoided. In deconstruction we try to notice what is not said, or at least some of what is not said, even in situations where the focus is upon what is said. When deconstructing, practitioner researchers feel themselves at a remove from what they are experiencing. They view the culture from a distance. Ways of seeing things in a familiar light now become unfamiliar. The purpose of deconstruction is to make transparent the limits of ideology. When inclusive practices are interpreted and analysed through action research, they are being deconstructed. We challenge the data and take it apart before we rebuild it through the written research record.

Values

Values refer to the worth or importance of something. Personally held values refer to the 'worth' or priority we bestow on what we believe to be valuable in life. We give our energy every day to doing everyday things – but we do this because we believe that the values from which we work are important, or are doing something positive for us or other people. We may do things for people who are close to us or family members – it is a kind of love that we show in doing these things. However, we may do things for other people because we get paid to, whom we may not love in the same way, but who need our professional help. Within these roles, when giving ourselves to others, there are attitudes and beliefs about the reasons for what we do, and how much reward there is in it for us. We feel a sense of worth in doing things; otherwise we feel less worthy ourselves. So, in order to function in the world we hold a set of beliefs and attitudes about our position in the world, and about how and what we can contribute to it – and at what cost. Values can be something of which we are aware, or they may be unconscious or implicit. In specific societies different values operate at a cultural level and are not evident to the 'insiders', i.e. members of the group, who hold and subsequently act out the cultural values they have absorbed in the 'group' culture. This is often the case with teachers and other educators.

However, in deconstructing and fully understanding what is happening in relation to inclusion, we need to sharpen our awareness of how our actions affect others and why other people act in the way that they do. If we are to influence the actions of others, we must understand our own actions and develop a full understanding of why they are 'valued' or 'devalued' as they are. So values are a function of cultures and groups as well as individuals. Values in cultures are implicit and cement the 'group' in their actions. However, to develop attitudes of change and to create a more flexible and inclusive society, actions need to be deconstructed to find their value base, e.g. in classroom practice. No society or group remains static, and change, when it occurs, should not take place because of powerful forces imposing their will on less powerful ones. Change should be possible on a democratic basis within groups and societies, and to be fully understood should be owned by individuals. An idea or theory that changes one person develops into something that influences others who come into contact with it, or the person or persons expounding it, as was the case with Meg's story. Explanation of the values that underpin new ideas or theories, or activities demonstrating them in inclusive practice, makes them amenable and more accessible to others because they can understand how the ideas have been created, where they are coming from and what values are explicit within them. Those others then have the power to accept or reject them. If they are not explicit it is much more difficult.

Trying to understand power relations in society is the single most challenging issue in making inclusion a reality. There are many hegemonies that have been attacked in recent decades (e.g. selective schooling based on ability tests) because time has been taken to stand back and deconstruct the situation and to perceive it from a different viewpoint. The arguments for changing the status quo are made clear and followers of the ideas are free to accept or reject them. The argument, however, must have some substance, with evidence in its support. Learning to make the arguments, learning how to use evidence in support of change and developing the discourse, publicly and democratically, in its support is the means of creating greater change. Often both sides claim similar values that can sway the argument, e.g. inclusive values, but they differ in the fundamental manner in which the issues are addressed. Is it from the perspective of the greater 'good' of the individual or that of the benefit of the 'group' as a whole, e.g. the peer group or classroom? Research based on these arguments provides evidence for their support or rejection. Yet such a simple distinction will lead to totally contradictory actions.

To overcome teacher researcher bias, honest declarations of value positions in relation to the research topic should be made. As a motivation for research, attitudes and biases may be useful, but paying attention to them during the research process will reveal one's implicit relationship with them. Recognizing one's values may be a liberating experience, freeing the person from the oppression of certain anchored beliefs, through a deeper understanding of the issues, leading to new attitudes, values or theories about. Overall, research with interpretive reflection and self-evaluation offers the possibility of revealing implicit assumptions and values, which are anchoring the person, preventing them from moving forward and professionally empowering them. The anchor chains may be freed through the process of deconstruction and reconstruction through action research. A reconstruction of the problematic situation is based on evidence, reflection and a democratic and inclusive interpretive discourse.

CHAPTER FOUR

Action and constraints

Action with a purpose is deliberate; it involves a consciously
foreseen end and a mental weighing of considerations pro
and con. It also involves a conscious state of longing or
desire for an end. The deliberate choice of an aim and of a
settled disposition of desire takes time.

(Dewey 1966: 347)

Action research is essentially an educational process, in which the researcher's
perception of the research focus changes during the investigative process.
The change may unconsciously or consciously motivate action for inclusive
practice in an innovative or novel direction. It may direct the teacher
researcher to find different ways of acting professionally because of a changed
awareness and a determination to make an impact on static or unproductive
educational contexts. Such change in the person is what makes the research
educational. It can provide a personal confidence and certainty that forms a
platform for planned and effective action. Action based on educational change
resulting from the research process is a form of planned voluntary action.
Before action is planned there must be an intention to make a change, and the
intention must be under voluntary control. An essential feature of planning
for action is the cooperation of others. Negotiation of the planned action
also depends on the reciprocation of others. When another person fails to co-
operate, a more compliant participant might have to be sought. Participation
needs to be negotiated and confirmed. Actions also need to be attempted for
successful completion of the research plan. However, when repeated efforts
to take the intended action fail, more fundamental reflection is necessary to
consider the reasons for failure and to plan alternatives.

Action research involves human agency that permeates the whole research
process through the activity of investigation itself. It requires active intervention in situations that need to be changed. Investigatory activities are
obviously essential in any research situation, but intervention and action
aimed at changing the situation are deliberate and intentional. Intentional
action is planned and organized with the aim of benefiting the research

participants through the implementation of improved inclusive practice. Because agency is essential in change, the case studies and stories in this book are used as practical examples of planned and active intervention by teachers in their own schools. Often teachers with limited time reach the stage of planning actions that they intend to implement later when the opportunity arises. However, they overlook the fact that the research methods they are using are in themselves a form of action. When action is merely planned, the research is incomplete. It is only when deliberate intervention is made and planned action is taken that the results can be monitored and evaluated.

For action to be successful it should be planned immediately prior to being taken. The shorter the delay, the more meaningful is the action, because of its immediate impact. The determination to take action is bolstered by beliefs about the likely consequences of success or failure, one's personal values and the motivation to remain strong in adverse and unexpected situations. Most people will attempt specific action if they believe that the advantages of success outweigh the disadvantages of failure, and if their personal values support the inclusive actions planned. We can never be absolutely certain that we will always be in a position to carry out our intentions; therefore, every intention is a goal whose success is uncertain.

We need to learn through knowing before we act. In order to act confidently in the many situations that present themselves in our lives, we must act on our previous learning, which is embodied in our assumptions and action in professional situations. We may not have time to examine assumptions lying behind our every action, but our assumptions should be clearly visible to our understanding of practice. We need to work from an explicit rather than an implicit theory of action. When a theory is made explicit, professionals have a better opportunity to test and evolve personal theories of their own to support their practices. (O'Hanlon 1995c).

The actions taken by professionals can be seen as role behaviour. Yet within the role taking is the identity of self. It is our identity that forms our awareness and our actions in 'any' or 'many' roles in life, including the teaching role. But human action is not intelligible if seen only as pushed from 'behind' or 'above', as deterministically caused. All action is intentional and has a future reference. Psychologists like Maslow (1987) see self-actualization as the ultimate need for the self to find expression. This pinnacle of human endeavour is based on personal values. A characteristic of Maslow's self-actualization is self-acceptance. Self-acceptance involves reconciliation with oneself and adverse circumstances and events in one's life (Jung 1998). The development of adults in educational contexts includes self-acceptance, self-awareness, self-evaluation and, ultimately, self-actualization. Successful role behaviour is facilitated by greater self-awareness and understanding of actions, achieved by making our theories of action explicit.

For example, Shona developed more self-awareness and confidence by remaining true to her individual needs and values. She began her research with every intention of transforming the urban school where she taught into a more inclusive school, but things turned out differently.

Shona began by investigating her urban primary school's response to children with different learning needs. She was the school coordinator for learning support. She spent a year gathering evidence about the school's practices and problems in implementing policy for these children. She met many barriers to her research, and consequently her proposed changes, which were always openly discussed with all the staff, were never fully implemented. After a frustrating school year acting as a practitioner researcher, she felt she was getting nowhere with attempts to improve school inclusion practice. She realized that she was not 'with' the staff in terms of attitudes, values and motivational energy. She was a 'doer', someone who wanted things to happen. Generally, the rest of the school staff were content to wait and take things as they came. Change did not appear to be on their agenda. Because of her realization that she was in a professional cul-de-sac, impotent to change the school culture, she applied for, and succeeded in obtaining, a post as vice-principal of a small rural school. She was concerned, because the focus of her action research would have to change in the following year. She was encouraged to keep a journal describing her new role, and found that she was experiencing dilemmas in relation to the role of vice-principal as agreed in the job description and interview. She was by now an experienced action researcher. She was competent at choosing appropriate research methods, gathering evidence, negotiating and discussing planned changes with a group of colleagues. After some time researching 'the balance of teaching and administration in the school', and holding frequent meetings with the headteacher about the delegation and sharing of tasks, she found time to plan and take action to prioritize the teaching of children who had different learning needs in the school. But this plan was not to be fully realized, because she had to interrupt her research priorities and focus on more pressing issues, related to practical school management concerns, before she could make any progress with her inclusion aims. She spent a year negotiating her role with the principal, through an action research process. She had been keeping a logbook of evidence of the constant requests made to her by the headteacher, many of which she saw as inappropriate and as interrupting her teaching. She succeeded in reaching an agreement with him about the boundaries of her administrative duties, which enabled her to concentrate on some quality time with pupils in need of additional help. Children with additional learning needs had previously been left to survive as best they could in the classroom with the other pupils. Shona organized their teaching programme and their additional learning support, and found quality learning time just for them in the everyday curriculum. She wrote up her action research investigation and its outcomes throughout the year.

Within a year, she was appointed to the position of headteacher. She claimed that action research had given her the confidence to understand herself professionally, to prioritize quality teaching time for pupils with different learning needs and to negotiate and discuss her present role with colleagues, based on evidence indicating the need for specific action for change.

The main point here is that Shona didn't succeed in the original aims of her action research in her urban school or in the succeeding year, but she dealt with what was necessary at the time, using an action research approach to realize her inclusive school aims successfully. This would not have been possible without the resolution of school pressures and the overcoming of school barriers that impeded her plans. She risked taking up a new school appointment because she couldn't create the change culture that she felt was necessary for success when her action research began in an urban school. Success was not sought simply in and for itself. Yet her aims were eventually realized in circumstances that were more appropriate to her assertive nature. She learned about herself by becoming reflexive with the aid of her journal, and used her new knowledge to make a difference in the rural school, where her experience and skills were valued. She found colleagues there who were responsive to her evidence and arguments. They boosted her self-esteem and validated her investigative plans to enable better inclusive practices. Although Shona was motivated to improve pupil learning in her first school, she found that colleagues didn't have the same impetus for change, and actively resisted it. Her planned action went beyond her original research topic into personal career moves, which led eventually to whole-school management issues.

The individual characteristics of researchers can influence the successful outcome of their intended action. Yet internal motivational factors are readily modifiable through training, experience and education. The most essential aspect of successful action is related to how people 'perceive' the extent to which they control their lives. Believing that social control and intervention are based on internal self-motivating factors encourages attempts to take professional action. Beliefs in personal control, or lack of control, over actions are related to whether or not professionals believe they possess certain personal attributes and characteristics necessary to perform the actions planned. Courage and conviction that one understands the situation and the need for change are often the starting point for successful action research.

Information, skills and ability are also necessary for successful action. It may require will-power or strength of character to implement specific action for inclusive practice, particularly in overtly political contexts like parliamentary practice, business, local government, educational institutions and schools. In his analysis of action and control, Kuhl (1982) has introduced the concept of *state* versus *action* orientation. A person's orientation is viewed as a relatively stable disposition and is dependent on a variety of situational factors. *Action*-oriented individuals make use of their knowledge and abilities to control what they do, whereas *state*-oriented individuals focus their attention on their thoughts and feelings, rather than taking action consistent with their plan or goal. Action-oriented individuals succeed in reaching their goals more than state-oriented individuals.

There is a resonance in this finding with Shona's reasons for leaving her first school, because she is clearly an action-oriented teacher. There are many individual attributes that tend to influence our control over action. For example, it is difficult fully to neutralize strongly held emotions, or compulsions to act in an unreflective manner. Yet it is important to understand the influence of intense emotions on our professional behaviour and intentions to act, and to find ways of accepting and controlling them.

Some changes occur naturally over time, while others are deliberate and intentional and depend on the emergence of new information or knowledge. In action research we rely upon evidence to provide new intentions or aspirations. A multitude of unanticipated events can disrupt the ability to reach a goal, leading to a revised goal. If aspirations for inclusive practice are held with great strength they are more likely to be successful. Researchers have found that attitudes held with high confidence are better predictors of action than attitudes held with low confidence (Sample and Warland 1973). The implication is that if teacher researchers really want improved inclusive practice they will succeed, but if they have been forced to implement inclusive practice, they may not make noticeable progress if they are reluctant, or have little belief or confidence in its success. However, it has been noted that the very act of stating an intention may induce heightened commitment to the action. Sherman (1997) found that respondents who predicted that they would act in a socially desirable manner were more likely to do so on a later occasion than respondents who were not asked to predict their actions. Therefore, the very act of discussing inclusive practice and considering its possibilities is an incentive to teacher researchers whose attitudes may be uncertain.

The following case study illustrates, in one instance, the way in which action research can develop inclusive school practice. Lynn is a teacher who is also a special educational needs coordinator. She attended an in-service course focused on 'inclusive school practice' through action research. She collected detailed evidence in the classroom and school, and spent time talking and negotiating with colleagues. She regularly shared her issues, problems and research evidence with course participants. Finally, she kept a detailed journal, which she used for personal reflection and for evidence of activities within the case itself.

This action research process involves reflection, data collection, reflection, planned intervention, reflection, taking action, reflection and evaluation. Lynn follows a set procedure for action research in her investigation of one child's inclusion in a mainstream classroom. She begins by identifying her research question, by asking herself whether it is possible for pupils to accept fully and include a member of their peer group who is isolated or unpopular. This particular case study is personally significant to the writer because of an incident that occurred in 1964.

It's a Friday morning in a second year classroom in a junior school situated in a large council housing estate in the suburbs of a large English city. The 48-eight pupils are seated in rows working in silence, copying out an exercise on pronouns from a textbook named *The Queen's English*.

The teacher is sitting behind a desk marking pupils' work. The teacher utters a loud sigh, looks up and calls out to a female pupil by name. The pupil approaches her desk. The teacher holds a sheaf of paper under the pupil's nose. 'What is this?', she asks. The pupil does not reply. The teacher leans in closer and shouts, 'What is this rubbish?' The pupil's eyes shine with unshed tears. 'My spelling corrections,' she mumbles. The teacher waves the sheaf of paper again. 'I asked you to write out each word 50 times to get it into your lazy head and look, look, you can't even copy them correctly!', she continues to shout.

The pupil looks at the waving papers in the adult's hand and notices that, at various points on the pages, words have been underscored with red pen. 'You are really the dullest, laziest girl I have ever taught!' The teacher then adds, 'Well, I'm not putting up with it!' She takes two thick wooden rulers out of the desk drawer and lines them up together. 'Hold out your hand,' she commands. The girl offers the palm of her right hand. 'No, the other one, stupid, you need that one to work with.' She is admonished. The pupil offers the palm of her left hand. 'Turn your hand over,' she is told. The teacher proceeds to rap the pupil across the knuckles of her left hand with six blows of the rulers. 'Let that be a reminder that your laziness will be punished,' the teacher comments, as she returns the rulers to the drawer. She concludes the interaction between them by saying, 'I despair of you, you'll never amount to anything. Now get back to your place and try not to make any more stupid mistakes.' The pupil, fighting back tears of humiliation and pain, walks scarlet-faced back to her seat. The class, who have been observing the incident in silence, drop their heads to their work, anxious not to catch the eye of the girl or the teacher.

This girl has now grown to become a teacher, who is working to prevent any similar incidents ever occurring again. In her early schooling she was exposed to many similar incidents, and subsequently became increasingly isolated from her classmates, who didn't want to be seen associating with the girl that 'Miss' didn't like. Lynn therefore begins her action research with a personal connection with the issue under investigation. She feels that these incidents ate away at her self-esteem and caused long-term damage. She is determined to prevent similar experiences occurring within her professional boundaries as a SENCO in a large urban primary school.

Many of the pupils who attend the school come from government designated areas of severe deprivation because of high unemployment, low levels of take-up for post-16 education, a high rate of teenage pregnancy and drug and alcohol abuse related crime.

Reflection. She begins with an awareness that several pupils in the school are not welcomed by their peer group in work or play situations. How can this situation be changed? This is her initial research issue. She defines her issue further through its confirmation by evidence from the existing situation. Her aim is to collect evidence of possible isolationist behaviour within the school and to unravel possible causes, e.g. bullying by adults or peers. She had been aware of comments made in the past by colleagues about a particular class group in the school and negative attitudes towards identified pupils in that class. In her role as SENCO, she is asked by a teacher to help with strategies to help one pupil from this class, who is viewed by staff as attention seeking, demanding and manipulative. She moves cautiously, as she wants to be sure about what is really taking place before she effects any changes for this pupil, who appears to be unhappy and unacceptable to his peer group. Does the school history of the pupil hold any clues to his present relationship? The incident that follows occurrs during the initial phase of the research.

It is Wednesday morning in a small primary school in rural England. The class of 33 pupils is clearing away after a practical number session.

The class teacher is engaged with two female pupils who are not sure how to convert 128 centimetres into 1 metre 28 centimetres. A volunteer helper is super-vising the collection of metre sticks and general tidying away. A pupil approaches the teacher and says, in an agitated manner, 'Miss, Miss, I had the metre stick first!' He then turns and attempts to snatch the stick from another pupil. The two boys then grapple with the stick. Mrs Jones (the helper) takes the stick from the boys and says aggressively, 'Sean, get back to your place, you are always causing trouble.' Sean protests, 'But I did have it first, Billy took it off me!'

Mrs Jones replies, 'I know all about you, Sean, any excuse to be a nuisance.'

Sean's face reddens, and he turns away and walks moodily back to his seat. Billy laughs a 'ha ha' and pokes his tongue out at Sean's back. Other pupils snigger.

The class teacher intervenes by standing and saying 'Thank you for your help, Mrs Jones. If we are ready I think it is playtime. I need to have a word with Billy and Sean before they go out to play.'

The class file out and the class teacher asks the two boys to join her on the comfy seats. She speaks, 'Well, Mrs Jones, we need to sort this out don't we, as you know what we always say about a fresh start every day?' She turns back to the boys. 'Now I think you both owe Mrs Jones an apology for squabbling over the metre stick.' The boys apologize sheepishly. 'Now, Billy,' she goes on, 'you owe Sean an apology for upsetting him, as I saw you snatching the stick from him when he was being helpful.'

Billy mumbles a reluctant apology to Sean. As he does so, the class teacher catches Billy's eye. Then she shoos the children out into the playground and invites Mrs Jones to join her for a coffee. They walk up the corridor together and the teacher is heard commenting to the helper, 'We need to give them all a fresh start this term as it too easy to fall into the trap of giving a dog a bad name.'

Investigation. The incident alerted Lynn to the possibility that adult attitudes could be contributing to Sean's behaviour and the attitude of his peers. This parent helper had worked with his year group in the previous year and it was possible that this may have coloured her perception of the child as he was now. She felt a challenge to find out about the inclusive nature of the school, and whether there was a history of adult–pupil interaction that could encourage or exacerbate the isolation of some pupils. To tease out these elements, she needed to find evidence of social exclusion taking place. She began the data collection by observing in the classroom. She observed a pupil who was seeking attention from adults and from peers, in a manner not always appropriate for the given situation. For example:

'Sean is doing the work set for the class during a mathematics lesson. Then he speaks to Billy across the table.

"Give me the colours."

Billy ignores him and goes on working. Sean gets out of his seat and calls out. "Mr Black, Billy isn't sharing the colours." Mr Black approaches the group. As he does so, Sean hurries round the table, grabs the pencil holder and leans over it, covering it with the top half of his body. Billy then attempts to pull the pencil pot away from Sean.

Mr Black calmly says, "You don't need those now, you haven't done the fives on the back yet. What you have done is very good, but you need to do the fives before you need the pencils."

Sean goes back to his place and resumes his work.'

Sean's attention seeking behaviour was not the sole reason for his isolation from his peer group. Notes from Lynn's journal indicate other problems.

'Sean appears to be unpopular. Evidence of this were the audible groans and "Oh no's" that were uttered when he was allocated to a new table group today. Katie cried when she knew he was in her table group. When she was asked why she was upset she replied, "We will never win any team points for good behaviour now." '

Other similar incidents were recorded during this initial phase of confirmation. Lynn wondered if he was the most unpopular pupil in his year group.

To answer this question she devised a sociogram with the help of other course colleagues, which was used in a lesson on 'invitations'.

The results of this data collection revealed that Sean was seen by almost half of the peer group as someone they would prefer not to work or play with. There were two other pupils who also appeared to be unpopular, but this was not always as evident during classroom situations, because they weren't treated in the same way as Sean. Sean seemed to be excluded from class and social activities for most of the school day. More evidence was found on the school's 'incident' forms, where it was confirmed that Sean was not the most frequent offender in his year group and that the class view of him as the 'naughtiest' boy was not justified. Lynn, at this time, had the opportunity to talk to Sean's parents. They reported that Sean had told them he was 'no good', and that he seemed to be unhappy about school. The parents traced the problem back to his first experiences of school, when they were met with a list of complaints about Sean's behaviour. Although they admitted he could be stubborn and demanding at times, he also became 'the reception teacher's whipping boy'. His mother claimed that he had given up on being good, because he felt no one noticed when he tried.

Planning and action. At this stage Lynn determined to offer some opportunities to effect change in Sean's situation. In discussion with Sean they agreed that when he felt the need to talk they would use a green card system. The green card meant 'green for go' and would be placed on his desk when he wanted to talk to the teacher. Lynn would acknowledge the card and arrange a meeting. They also introduced a behaviour card with only smiley faces on it. This, it was agreed, was to go home with at least one positive comment every day. Weekly meetings were set up with Sean's mother and Sean, and although sometimes it was tough, they always focused on the things he had done well.

Because the 'incidents' of concern involving Sean were more frequent during break times, Lynn arranged, in negotiation with Sean, to choose a midday supervisor who would oversee his behaviour and report back to Lynn every lunchtime.

As a consequence of these interventions to help Sean, Lynn developed a close working relationship with his parents, who agreed that he would also receive help with his social skills and work on his self-esteem. This takes place on two afternoons a week and his parents are very pleased with his progress. His is calmer and more controlled in the classroom, and is trying to stop himself making inappropriate interruptions to the teacher.

The issue about peer group acceptance was a more difficult one. Lynn introduced several games to enhance self-esteem to the whole class group. As a consequence of this, a class peer described Sean as 'always helpful if you are upset, kind to others, he helps me with my work and is daring'.

Lynn sensed that the parents also felt isolated because of their concerns about Sean. She invited the LEA 'parent partnership' team to meet with parents at the school to explain their role. The outcome of the meeting was that a small group of parents, including Sean's mother, have set up their own school support group and planned a number of social evenings and discussions, including one about 'behaviour management at home'.

The issue of changing the attitudes of colleagues is to be a long-term project for future investigation. However, in-service days have been arranged for teachers and supervisors, who are to receive training in dealing with 'difficult' children.

The school management team have been alerted to the problems that need to be addressed school-wide and have agreed to a revision of the school's policy on bullying and to finding ways of putting the 'Inclusion Index' into practice. The appointment of pupils to the management team is still an issue to be resolved.

As a postscript to the research, Lynn notes that she was given the opportunity to reflect on her practice and to understand better what 'inclusion' means in everyday terms. She focused on one particular pupil, to investigate and question the inclusive nature of the school itself. It is clear after this action research study that there is more work to be done to encourage a more inclusive ethos in the school and classroom, and barriers need to be broken down where negative attitudes persist. Lynn has gained a renewed confidence in her role as SENCO through all her discussions with staff in the school and her deeper awareness of the reasons for low staff morale and high stress levels among teaching staff. She is now training as a facilitator in community support, and acknowledges that this is not something she would have done without the growth in her personal development that the action research has encouraged.

Lynn's case study is notable because she was able to complete it within a three to four month period. Time was short, yet she attempted to change the school's inclusive culture by beginning in the classroom, observing what was actually taking place. She selected from her observation data a number of incidents concerning Sean that she felt were relevant to her research. It is never possible to include all the research data in any action research project. Sean was seen by her to be isolated from his peers. Yet she had to confirm this assumption through the collection of evidence. She found that staff responses to his behaviour were inconsistent, depending on who was 'on the spot' at the time. She felt that preconceived attitudes to Sean were colouring staff responses, which she attempted to challenge. Lynn had to go beyond the classroom situation to discuss the behaviour and more appropriate responses to it by taking time to talk to the parent helper and Sean's parents. As often happens in action research, her research brief widened to involvement with parents, which was not initially anticipated.

A plan of action was devised to improve Sean's behaviour directly, as well as challenging staff and peer attitudes and responses to him. Lynn included Sean in discussions about what was planned. She also developed a plan to involve Sean's classmates in a more positive and constructive attitude to him, to break down his apparent isolation from them. She found time to talk to school colleagues to encourage discussion of her problems and to involve them in a process of understanding and approval of her plans.

She kept a research journal using headings like 'About me', 'Colleagues' responses and comments', 'Parents', 'Classroom observations and incidents', 'Reflection' and 'Action to be taken' (see Chapter 8). She realized through her journal reflection that any small action to improve inclusive practice is helpful, although more time would achieve more school-wide change than occurred. Nevertheless, she was determined to continue to investigate on a 'whole school' basis through the provision of help and training for staff dealing with 'difficult' children. She has, in this case, prevented an escalation of the situation related to Sean's behaviour, and possible school exclusion. Lynn's case study is abbreviated in the above account. It was accompanied by detailed evidence, questionnaires to staff, classroom observation, reflective detail from the journal and commentary and planning feedback from friends, colleagues and action research group members.

Advantages and constraints in the process of action research

The advantage of using an action research approach is that an active case study of one's own practice can be developed. The professional's role can be improved through the implementation of improved inclusive practices with the support of a friend, colleague, tutor or research or collegial group. Passionate concerns and priorities in inclusive practice can be investigated through the collection of evidence as a basis for deliberate change, particularly in situations believed to be non-inclusive. The impact of the action will depend upon the power of the action and its intended effects. It offers an opportunity to change society and its institutions through the direct agency of those most directly concerned with bringing about an inclusive educational community.

The constraints in action research depend upon the quality and depth of the evidence (or lack of), the rigour of the data interpretation and the openness of the practitioner researcher and research participants to accepting and understanding hidden assumptions and power issues within the dynamics of the situation. The opportunity to discuss the evidence, investigatory methods and ethics of procedures is critical to the success of the action research project. Action researchers are field workers in education who make an impact on the situation, while also acknowledging the success or failure of their efforts. The research project itself may fail if the teacher researcher is unwilling to take action or to confront the educational dilemmas found in the real world of educational practice. It may also fail if the teacher researcher is not prepared to be totally honest and self-critical and to see himself or herself as a director of the action, with inherent power to effect change in the ongoing investigation and its outcomes. Power is not equally balanced in the research situation, where some participants may be more involved and in control than others. The constraints of action research also lie within the authentic motives, attitudes, understanding and intentions of the principal researcher, and his or her ability to conceptualize and understand the wider political implications of the research.

Hoyle (1974) makes a distinction between professionalization (connected to status) and professionalism (connected to quality of practice). This distinction differentiates between the role and its status, and both are related to how individual professionals respond to the need to develop better practice. Teacher researchers carrying out action research for inclusion are primarily developing their professionalism, but they may incidentally improve their professional status in the process. The quality of practice in professionalism emphasizes the individual's obligations in the role. Obligations must be personally accepted before they can be actualized in practice. How do professionals meet goals for inclusion and social justice if their obligations are not already held on a personal level?

Attempts to change the person within the professional role may meet with personal resistance, because the change affects both the professionalization and professionalism of the person's practice. There are many professionals who attempt the process of action research for professional development with little conviction for change. They may refuse to search for, or accept, better or more comprehensive explanations for their individual commitment to habitual and routine professional behaviour. There may be the belief that, although choices in action for inclusive practice exist objectively out there, external or structural factors are determining and possibly constraining the individual's actions, and this belief elicits emotional reactions of resistance. A teacher's refusal to change within the role might be justified with theories or ideas taken from psychology, sociology or education, or what is alleged to be common sense. There may be an allegedly objective description of the school or classroom situation that shows the professional in a favourable light. The investigative descriptions of issues may be unconsciously made, and not intended to be dishonest, as they form an 'identity' prop for the person. Yet if the view was revised or challenged, the teacher would be forced into a painful revision of their role, e.g. realizing that when teaching she is too dominant in classroom discussion, which leads to pupils' fearful rather than spontaneous responses.

There is also the problem of false consciousness, i.e. the mistaken beliefs shared and held by educators about the nature and function of their role, which may be the result of misinformation or inadequate knowledge.

The way to overcome many of these constraints is to develop democratic and inclusive participation in action research. We need to consider how we model inclusive values like opening access and creating equal opportunities for participants who contribute to the investigative process. In the research and interpretive discourse a new explanation of events and the modification of educational traditions support a transparent awareness and consciousness, through the community development of inclusive practice.

CHAPTER FIVE

Collaboration, a democratic and inclusive process: penetrating the black diorite

The idea of sitting down together and seriously discussing educational purpose and how it might be achieved is not typically found in the teachers' lounge . . . Teachers who are researchers share their findings with one another, discuss interpretations of the findings, and work together to implement strategies based on new understandings which emerge . . . Teachers who are researchers are much more likely to recognise the socially deleterious effect of certain educational strategies than non-researching teachers.

(Kincheloe 1991: 5)

Collaboration with a friend, colleague or group is important to ensure the quality of action research for inclusive practice. Collaboration to develop democratic, discursive and inclusive practice to support change is not simply a matter of telling someone else what you are doing or what you are planning to do. It depends on interaction with one or more persons on the basis of evidence, reflection, debate and plans for active change. Participants must make a personal choice about whether they will contribute on this basis. Collaboration is voluntary. It may be informal and requires a commitment to the inherent aims of the investigation.

The term democratic participation is used in this book to refer to a system in which decisions are taken and policies created, as a result of the widest possible free and open discourse. Central to the effective working of Greek democracy was the idea of active citizenship. The success of the democracy depended upon citizens accepting their civic responsibility and sustaining a sense of identification with the future of their culture, which they actively pursued. 'In a democracy, effective action must necessarily be based on voluntary contribution . . . taking place through the arts of persuasion and influence' (Mill

1929). The value of participatory experience lies in the encouragement of people to exercise independent judgement, enabling them and forcing them to take a public stand on issues stimulating a political dialectic, which if it does not result in improved politics may result in improved persons. Therefore, if greater inclusion is not achieved through our actions, perhaps one's personal character and reputation may be enhanced. Greater participation and further democratization is an agenda for interpretation and investigation, as well as for political action.

The ideas and strategies spelled out in this book are based on a person's professional need to be part of an educational culture that uses its inherent agency for the benefit of marginalized individuals and groups. Democratic participation encourages all the participants to contribute and be respected and valued equally throughout the research process. Inclusive principles are affirmed, with the visibility of democratic research procedures inherent in its actions, conversations and discussions.

In practice, equal valuing of contributions from research participants, colleagues or members of a research group depends on the skill to listen. Other interactional skills are:

- monitoring how much you talk and lead the conversation;
- how much you wait for another to respond or comment;
- asking appropriate questions;
- paraphrasing information you have received for clarification and to check meaning;
- reiterating your understanding of what has been said;
- clearly explaining your interpretation of others' data;
- providing a balance of talk among participants that focuses on individual members when they are allocated time to share and discuss their data.

The discourse around the investigation requires listening to others, and responding to their concerns, rather than relating similar events that have occurred in your life, or offering helpful advice about what you think needs to be done, before the issue has been thoroughly investigated and discussed. There is a temptation to find a right answer to the concerns that are raised, yet there are many possibilities. It is important to focus on actual evidence and data, recognizing them as different from opinions or inferences, which are more a form of personal interpretation. The use of questioning is essential when the discussion becomes bogged down, and is generally a good strategy when participants are unclear about the direction of the discourse.

Collaborators and participants need to share the inclusive aims of the investigation, and responsibility for crucial decisions. Discussions with collaborators and participants will support difficult decision-making and planning for active intervention and change. The responsibility for the outcomes must be part of a mutual commitment to the consequences. The discursive relationships based on trust and mutual respect make personal and ideological challenges more acceptable in an open and honest atmosphere.

Collaboration involves:

- developing democratic, inclusive, discursive practice;
- voluntary participation;
- shared values and aims;
- equal participation;
- good listening skills;
- shared responsibility for decision-making;
- mutual trust and respect.

The creation of collaborative relationships requires a deliberate intention to communicate with others to realize the ideals for an inclusive research study. They build up a rapport through interaction, which becomes more confident when trust is built up in partnership with others. Changing situations to make them more inclusive involves political intervention that may change the status quo. This requires courage and conviction built up from an interpretive and democratic discourse.

An awareness of the political power of the change process is vital to the participants' understanding of the process of empowerment. What consequences should we expect from deliberately influencing organizations to change and widen access to learning by encouraging wider social and educational inclusion? What professional and political skills do teachers need to convince others of the value of their investigations, and how do they acquire them? Change through action research requires heavy professional and political investments by teacher researchers in a climate that is generally unfavourable because managerial and contractual relationships are enshrined in contact hours, with performance indicators and other forms of accountability. Such constraints may undermine the kind of professional commitment that action research relies upon. Action research has the possibility of being transformative when collaboration and focus are strong, but it may operate on the margins if the process is deflected or diminished by lack of commitment or loss of direction. Action research works best when located in a collaborative political paradigm that generates local and personal knowledge that can be translated into the leverage of power. The power is inherent in the new knowledge, the redefinition of the problems and the changed recognition of the teachers. How do we judge the political effectiveness of the research? How do we ensure its success? By situating teachers at the centre of the action and supporting them in a discursive interpretation of the barriers to social and educational inclusion, they can be established as key players in educational change. The existing educational ideology can be changed and transformed by teachers' practice. Action research tries to identify contradictions between educational and institutional practices and thus creates a self-critical community of action researchers. The attempt to change existing institutional barriers is political action that aims to provide a basis for overcoming educational injustice, alienation and deprivation.

A group process: interpretive discourse

Teacher researchers and other research participants may decide to form a group that meets to discuss the data, its implications, interpretation and planned action. This may be formally or informally convened. Formal action research groups are often formed in parallel with higher degree courses in universities, e.g. the formation of a group based on democratically agreed rules, the membership of which is entirely voluntary. The formal support group may not involve direct teaching or tutoring, but can provide a venue for wider debate of research methodology, ethical issues and decision-making for change. It provides a form of educational scaffolding for a more secure research process.

There may be many times during the sorting and sifting of evidence when teachers or researchers feel their research project or thesis will never be organized or completed. It often helps to share these feelings with others who are in the same situation. It can be helpful to agree that an equal amount of time be devoted to each member of the group to discuss their own particular issues, and an agenda can be prepared in advance for the sharing of journal writing, notes, ideas, useful literature sources and contentious issues. The group may devise procedural rules, such as:

* listen carefully to each presenter;
* take notes of what is said;
* challenge each other's unreflective assumptions in an assertive, but non-aggressive or personal, manner;
* think *for* the person talking rather than *about* them;
* address the speaker's behaviour and practice, rather than personal foibles or characteristics;
* aim to create a trusting and 'confidential to the group' atmosphere;
* demonstrate that the discourse and rhetoric are creating new knowledge.

The resolution of research issues in a discussion group may lead to increased motivation for change, because colleagues encourage and coax each other, but it may also lead to tension. When barriers constantly thwart our efforts, we may feel an increased need to change the situation to make it more comfortable for us. 'When all ways are barred and we have to act, an unbearable tension is set up in us, we therefore try to change the world, reconstitute it or transform it' (Sartre 1957). It is up to the group members to decide how to transform their world, or to make it more comfortable for them to tolerate. However, if the researcher feels an unbearable tension, a certain destabilizing of their former foundations and beliefs, the only course of action may be to retreat. A position of retreat may be obvious when the researcher uses artificial or borrowed issues. However, maintaining this position of deception is difficult when one is a member of a challenging discussion group, because in any dialogue there is an element of truth. Thoughts are a reflection of reality. All ideas, even the most apparently false and erroneous of them, reflect reality in some fashion and contain a measure of truth. Every person will transmit something of their own reality through the debate and discussion. It is the responsibility of group members to foster mutual trust, to expose underlying assumptions and unrecognized emotions that may constrain the honest exchange of views. A position of retreat is the ultimate refusal to act. The group's sensitivity to this position may not prevent colleagues from reaching their destination through a safer route, but the group support will inevitably extend its members' self-understanding in a process that may involve taking professional risks.

Collaboration

Action research involves individuals studying social and educational situations in which the participants inquire and learn by observing and questioning each other at first hand. The success of the endeavour, like that of any interaction, is dependent on the willingness and ability of the research participants to establish a meaningful basis for communicating. Consulting colleagues or joining an action research group prevents the action research from becoming one-sided and selfish, because it has its inception in the mind of one individual who may unilaterally decide which specific individuals or groups will serve as an evidential resource. Decisions to use specific information sources, and to reject others because they may not be beneficial to the research, are best shared before action is implemented. What to investigate, whom to include and how to carry it out, should be decided in consultation with another or others, rather than individually.

If the decision is made to proceed with the original research question or issue, then one is confronted with the tasks of functioning as a researcher and accepting the responsibilities that the role entails. The nature of these responsibilities is dependent upon the intention of the action research project to be implemented. The research may call for one to operate as an 'unknown observer' and to test implicit or explicit hypotheses, by observing others without their knowing that their behaviour is under scrutiny. This often happens when teachers observe pupils in schools. However, the task of beginning to function as a researcher involves more than conditioning oneself to observe systematically and to document what one has perceived. It also entails gaining the understanding and cooperation of the people who have been chosen to provide much needed data and information for the research. Often children and young people have not been approached for their consent prior to the research. It is taken for granted that, as actors in the social situation, their presence and actions may be observed and monitored, particularly if they are perceived as having low social status. Yet it is not democratic or inclusive action research unless participants fully understand their rights and the researcher accepts the responsibility to protect their rights.

Establishing a structure for initiating interaction, whether by oneself or with the help of intermediaries, is essential for implementing research plans that depend upon the collaboration of others. To gain the cooperation of others, however, researchers must be able to explain their purposes and expectations meaningfully and convincingly. How do they do so, and what are the responses likely to be?

It is important to establish the best possible climate for participation, and to establish rapport with others involved in the research right from the start. Once rapport has been established, the research can get under way. However, there may be confrontations that occur at the moment of encounter, and continue throughout the duration of the research. Rapport has to be negotiated continuously, as the context for the research is constantly changing. This is similar to many other kinds of human interaction: as the persons involved learn more about each other, trust can be better established and threats reduced, and the nature of interrelationships evolves and changes. However, there are dilemmas involved in establishing rapport by promising the participants shared control of the project, and in negotiating the inclusion of private and shared knowledge in public accounts. A democratic structure for the research may be in conflict with the political aims (Simons 1987). Moreover, democratic research and case studies may be simply incompatible with short time scales. This is a problem shared by teachers doing action research and is referred to by Elliott (1991) in his reflections of insider researchers on the dilemmas they face in doing action research in schools, raising issues about 'authority', 'privacy' and 'territoriality'. He suggests that teachers who have a problem finding time to undertake research could develop *creative resistance* to organizational constraints on their prioritizing of time, e.g. by refusing to be co-opted into organizational maintenance roles that undermine the development of reflective practice. Hence, there is a necessity for secure controls for participants in case studies, such as a formal contract of some kind that is binding upon participants. Participants cannot have the right to privacy and the public the right to know with respect to the same data. Yet it cannot be left entirely to the participants to make judgements related to private and public interest. It is for the evaluator or the principal researcher to judge what should become public. This becomes clearer when a distinction is made between social as opposed to educational evaluation. Social evaluation addresses the public right to know, whereas educational evaluation has the aim of sharing knowledge among educational professionals.

In a situation where participants make varied and exclusive judgements about what should be made known, an intermediary or broker can be invited in to negotiate when contention arises. Such a person might be one solution to the problem of bland, desensitized case study accounts that make no political impact on a readership beyond the participants (Simons 1987). In the action research process participants may, however, act as intermediaries for each other. Disagreements over what is written in the research record should be briefly acknowledged in the completed case study, perhaps in an appendix if not in the main account.

Anyone undertaking any form of research, particularly action research or case study, should be aware of the importance of:

- setting agreed democratic and inclusive procedures from the start;

- alerting participants to the nature of taking high risks and their consequences;
- discussing the nature of the terms 'openness', 'confidentiality' and 'participatory control';
- being aware of the tendency of researcher and participants to manipulate the data during the process of developing the account or research record;
- providing the opportunity to expose hidden agendas held by researchers, case study workers and participants;
- finding a means, within the methodology, of opening up process issues in an unthreatening manner;
- understanding the complex nature of obligations involved in developing action research for inclusion.

Ownership

There is always a struggle in the dialogue between individuals and the dominant culture. Bakhtin (1981) believes that when discourse is active those involved in it hear and learn about other's beliefs and thus develop their own 'ideological becoming'. He means that we confirm our beliefs and judgements through others' discourse. He maintains that an authoritative word, such as government policy, is hard to change when it is transmitted but not represented, i.e. created in dialogue with participants or recipients. He believes that everyone eventually forms their own beliefs and ideas and accepts what they want from the discourse of the authoritative word. The creation and maintenance of debate about inclusive practice enables participants to adopt their own ideological position and to situate it in the wider 'authoritative word' of policy and school directives that may not always have been created through consultative discourse.

There is an issue of research agendas for inclusive practice that are imposed from elsewhere. When a research agenda is imposed the results may be short-lived, because the research aims are not fully valued or owned by the research participants. This happens because action research may be used as a form of evaluation or audit in some school contexts.

An imposed agenda for inclusion within the school may close off areas for potential study; personal agendas may not be considered or invited. The managerial hierarchy and existing school structure can be reaffirmed through undemocratic school change and improvement.

Research that proceeds unaware of the micropolitical strategies within the process is featureless. It renders much of what is achieved as questionable, in terms of real structural or political change within the school, if democratic or inclusive ideas are not modelled in the process itself. Teachers may not always be given the opportunity to question the authority for establishing school evaluation procedures, or to confront them if they find it unnecessary.

When the question of 'whose decision counts?' is asked, the response should enquire 'on what evidence is the decision based and is there a democratic decision-making process involving those most closely concerned?' When action is not viewed as a socially liberating and dynamic praxis, but as something done by activist groupings in which precise short-term goals are set, action research is a form of narrow pragmatism, often under the control and direction of state agencies and monitored by researchers. There is a danger that action research may become a form of social engineering that is antithetical to the action research process if it is not freely created and democratically developed.

These concerns are raised because of the erroneous assumption that action researchers need not always be personally involved in the investigation and reflection on their practice. They can be removed by ensuring that action research is not merely treated as a technical process. Ownership of the process and the empowerment of participants depend upon the research topic and its development, which:

- become the responsibility of the principal researcher(s) and participants;
- engage the participants in personal reflection, self-evaluation and self-awareness through a democratically controlled research process;
- use personal journals or diaries that are integral to the research, providing opportunities for participants to share their thoughts and reflections with colleagues and other participants, when appropriate;
- create a record of personal change in parallel with the 'case record' or case study, which recognizes personal change as an important aspect of professional and situational change;
- allow participants the right to edit their own contributions.

It is debatable just how far action research accounts and case studies have been, or should be, exposed to the wider public beyond the immediate research context and its participants. Many apolitical studies have been dumbed down for publication and wider dissemination in an effort to protect their participants. It is traditional in many higher education institutions to emphasize the professional and technical nature of the action research process at the expense of the more intimate personal developments and changes, which if they were included would render the accounts real, live, dramatic, powerful and dynamic. Research records that include biography and autobiography are interesting because of their inherent humanity, directness and immediate impact.

The recognition of feelings in professional practice is the first step in recognizing one's own values, and their importance in everyday activities. There is inevitably some emotional involvement in a process of change (O'Hanlon 1997). However, it is also possible to carry out action research without this recognition. There is always the danger of allowing the process of action research to improve only teachers' technical skills, such as time management. Narrow technical forms of action research are in danger of reinforcing existing power relations and hierarchies in education. We need to become more aware of 'how' we carry out action research to model the political values of democratic choice, inclusion and participation. The teacher researcher's awareness of the political nature of research is critical to changing the existing educational system for improved inclusive practice. The process needs to be conceived as both action research *for* inclusive practice and action research *as* inclusive practice.

In conclusion, collaboration with research participants in a democratic framework creates an inclusive research process. Participants must be invited to contribute on the basis of transparent aims and procedures. Everyone is equally respected, although there may need to be some resolution of conflict, perhaps involving a research intermediary who is mutually acceptable to both parties in a dispute. The micropolitical activities that are initiated for the purposes of inclusive practice are no less fundamental simply because they lie in the control of research participants who may not occupy high status professional roles. Political action carries an element of personal risk, yet it is rare for participants in the action research process to feel any regret about their actions when weighed against their enormous gains.

CHAPTER SIX

Methods and techniques in action research

Reflection is the appropriation of our effort to exist and of
our desire to be, through the work which bears witness to
that effort and desire.

(Sigmund Freud, quoted in Ricoeur 1970: 46)

In action research a number of methods are used for gathering data. Action
research includes all research methods that provide evidence that is relevant to
developing inclusive and educational practice. Action research predominantly
uses ethnographic methods, e.g. interviewing, because it involves people
with 'insider' or familiar knowledge of the situation, but any evidence that
informs the situation is acceptable. Action research acknowledges that the
researcher and participants hold individual perspectives that may influence
the direction of their research. Claims about the validity and authenticity of
action research depend upon those engaged in the research becoming aware
of the personal interests and values that shape this engagement. Values
and interests condition all research, but this is rarely acknowledged. In
action research researchers can identify an intrinsic self-referential attitude
that can be controlled by: first, acknowledging and recognizing individual
unique perspectives and possible covert attitudes inherent in the research
issues; second, widening, deconstructing and reconstituting them through
multiple perspectives in relation to the evidence collected. However, Feyerabend (1975) reminds us that when we consider theory and methodology,
experimentation and creativity are crucial to progress. Most scientific developments have occurred because people have unwittingly broken the established
rules or decided to abandon them because of their constraints. Action research
is at its best when seen as an exploratory methodology, which allows one to try
out new forms of investigation, with appropriate justification for their specific
validation and use.

The essential question for the researcher when deciding on methods is
whether the data gathering techniques will:

- confirm that the research topic (issue or question) is genuinely an immediate concern for oneself and others in the professional situation;
- elicit data necessary to deepen understanding of the research topic;
- contribute to multiple perspectives;
- be accepted and managed easily within the collaborative research framework;
- provide an honest, authentic account of the research focus and its investigative process;
- be appropriate for the inclusion, understanding and feedback of more vulnerable individuals and groups;
- be sensitive to the vulnerabilities of contributors and participants.

Action research employs a range of specific methods and techniques in addition to those that are well used in educational research. The most essential method in action research as outlined in this book is *interpretive discourse*, which occurs when research participants, colleagues or interested parties meet to form a core or focus group concerned with the investigation of a specific topic like inclusive practice. The process evolves in the dynamics of the investigation, through interpretive discourse and conversation. Data and evidence are collected and interpreted through a number of the following techniques, which are chosen for their appropriateness to teachers with only a basic training in research methods.

Interpretive discourse and conversation

Action research is always collaborative, because it cannot be developed without the contributions of others. It involves discussion and conversations, i.e. discourse with colleagues and participants, which can be seen as both a method and a methodology (Feldman 1995). Hollingsworth (1997) refers to the discursive process as collaborative conversation, which continues a long tradition from the ancient Greeks to the postmodern. A conversation is often an informal interchange between at least two people, which allows them to get to know each other better, share feelings, beliefs and values, past history and current ideas. In an action research context this becomes a formal or informal discourse with direction and meaning. It may not lead to the resolution of all controversial issues, but it will deepen understanding of what is desired when intentions for inclusive actions are aired.

Any discourse or conversation must, by its nature, be collaborative, because it needs at least two people who speak and listen to each other. A conversation is a meaning-making process, which leads to decision-making, the exchange of knowledge and the generation of understanding. It is claimed that conversations used for these purposes are a form of research in themselves. Conversation can be a form of inquiry, which can develop into systematic critical inquiry. When made public, this becomes a form of collaborative action research. Conversation is cooperative, an exchange of views, a dialogue between at least two people in a joint activity. There are no rules for conducting conversations, or for engaging in discourse and discussion that is interpretive, inclusive and democratic in form. What is important is that people engage with each other to share information that is relevant and truthful, and as directly as possible to convey meaning. The discourse does not always have to convince others about the truth or right of what is discussed. Discourse bonds or divides its speakers through agreement, or dissension, related to the social and political issues of inclusion. In action research, the conversations and discourse may become more organized in terms of time and place, but, nevertheless, they comprise collaborative inquiry in action. The rules of the discourse are created by its participants in the process of sharing investigatory evidence, concerns and planned action.

Process dynamics

In action research the participants negotiate a process that may involve them in interactive data collection that goes beyond the boundaries of traditional research. Participant research is inclusive too, because it inevitably means seeking the views and perceptions of its contributors: it involves the teacher researcher in interaction with contributors and participants, which changes the research dynamics, either temporarily or permanently depending on the form of intervention used. All researchers influence the existing situation through their intervention, and teacher researchers acknowledge this influence and change as an aspect of the situation that needs their attention, awareness and sensitive response. The action research account should describe how the intervention(s) influenced the situation, how the teacher researcher is perceived, e.g. as an 'outsider' or 'insider' in the situation, and how the research process affects the question or inclusive issue under investigation. A record of the changes brought about by the interactional dynamics and interventions (in a journal) may be seen as additional data for the research study, but is essential for an authentic account of the research process. It records the influences and changes that result from an action research process (see Chapter 8). The process dynamics are an aspect of research that are rarely acknowledged, but they are essential to an understanding of how successes or failures occur in reality. Often, teacher researchers are refused entry to institutions or access to essential information. They may experience difficulty in implementing planned changes, necessitating a revision of intended action, because of factors beyond their control. Research involving personal encounters, e.g. interviews, discussions and triangulation of data, also requires negotiation and the agreement of participants about how the research evidence should be represented. These decisions and agreements normally occur during the ongoing investigation, but may delay progress if dissension arises. What facilitates or obstructs the investigation is not a peripheral methodological issue, it is essential data for the understanding of procedural and methodological practices in research projects. It provides necessary information for the interpretation of power and control issues within the investigation itself. Teacher researchers should be prepared to make active responses to problems and issues that arise unexpectedly in the course of investigation. An interim report with evaluative feedback may be necessary to reassure participants before progress can be made to a successful conclusion.

The evidence will guide practice and inquiry, via reflection and evaluation, integrating the research and the practice into one process for the implementation of educational inclusive practice.

This process is developed through the following:

- research and investigation;
- applying theories and ideas through planning and action;
- evaluating practice, and evaluating practice as inclusive;
- involving colleagues and others in planning and making changes;
- reflection and discussion, the sharing of evidence and its interpretation;
- a continuous reframing and transforming of practice through the above process, which leads to a constant habitual evaluative change process involving the researcher and research participants.

The first thing that teacher researchers or professionals experience is a conscious raising of awareness built on the questions 'What am I doing?' and 'Why am I doing it?' or the statement 'I want to talk about my practice and reflect about why I am here.' In this first stage, they go through a phase of self-direction and self-awareness. During this time they may identify theories of practice. They may refer to 'grand theory', such as that of Piaget, Bruner, Vygotsky and other well known educational theorists. Yet to make a difference to individual situations, they need to understand and develop more personalized theories of inclusive practice, because everyone has an educational theory that they personally understand in a very real and practical sense. Personal theories, when brought to light through action research, can overturn what were thought to be sound theoretical ideas established in initial professional training courses. For example, when teacher researchers examine their own evidence they may find surprising contradictions related to previously held theories of language development (O'Hanlon 1992). The changes in teachers' beliefs and values, when validated and shared through participant and interpretive discourse, become more powerful because of personal recognition and attachment. Opening up the evidence in a situation where challenges are made and ambiguity is aired with colleagues who face similar contradictions and dilemmas provides individual teacher researchers with mutual group support.

Associated research techniques

Observation

Observation is a primary research method in action research. The teacher researcher is the main protagonist and in his or her professional role collects evidence to stimulate action to support specific inclusive goals. The researcher doesn't need to gain access to another culture to establish rapport, because he or she is already situated within the educational culture in multiple professional roles. In this respect, observation in the context of action research differs from participant observation as a method of outsider research. There is a difference between observations made by the teacher practitioner and those made by a collaborating outsider, even if it is a professional peer. The collaborating peer could be an 'ousider' in the specific locational context of the observation, e.g. the collection of teaching data from a colleague's classroom. All observational data should be collected openly and without deception. Once the research focus has been decided, the observation of certain situations can be planned. Observation may begin in a general context, e.g. the school or classroom, to confirm that the topic is appropriate and amenable to investigation. The selection of data to illuminate the topic is the first concern. Questions will include:

- What useful data can be collected?
- Who needs to participate in the observations?
- How should the evidence be recorded? When? How much?
- How should one interpret and report it?
- When and how do you discuss and share the evidence?

Technical support may be necessary, and this resource should be included in observational plans. The observer should have a clear idea of what is to be observed and recorded from the outset. The interpretation, semi-permanent and permanent records made subsequently should reflect a democratic and inclusive commentary of the process. Selected colleagues, with a little observational training, will prove a valuable resource to triangulate data or to record what is required in a non-technical and human way.

Techniques for observation include: interval recording, duration recording, frequency count recording, continuous recording and time sampling.

Duration recording refers to the use of a timing device or stop watch to measure time intervals between, for example, the occurrence of target behaviour, and time on or off task. The technique can be used to measure several behaviours related to one person or several people occupied in one behaviour. Reliability is obtained by the correlation of two observers' scores. Interobserver reliability can be gauged through a computational correlation of the scores if necessary.

Frequency count recording counts the target behaviour each time it occurs. Frequency counting is most useful in recording behaviours of short duration and those where the length of time taken is not important. Interobserver reliability can be gauged in the above manner.

Interval recording records the target behaviour at a given interval. The length of interval varies with the nature of the behaviour being observed. The behaviour is usually matched to a prepared inventory of expected behaviours. Both the sequence and frequency of behaviour can be tallied in this way.

Continuous recording is when all the behaviour of a target person is observed in each session or possibly for a day, a week or longer. It is not always possible to record everything, but focusing on specific relevant behaviours is essential for planning and interpreting the observational data. This is a much-used method in educational research.

Time sampling is the selection of specific time periods for observation from the total time available. The intervals may be selected on a systematic basis or at random. A researcher could choose a common teacher behaviour like classroom management, and select one hour during the day in which to observe it. Alternatively, the behaviour to be observed may be pupil control at break time and play. A fixed period of observation would then be chosen.

The teacher researcher builds up evidence over time, making sense of the main issues and making logical connections between the data. These connections can be tested against new data and may be modified and refined before the next stage of data collection. Data are collected to confirm the data connections, but it is also imperative to collect data that disconfirm alternatives. It is a one-sided research exercise that does not seek to disprove or invalidate an antithetical research proposition.

Progressive focusing is the systematic confirmation of data against basic assumptions and the elimination of irrelevant data. It is a move from the empirical to the conceptual through making inferential connections. How do we validate the process?

- By constantly checking evidence with participants involved in the research study through techniques like triangulation (see below).
- By involving others in judgements about the trustworthiness of the data.
- Through evaluation of the quality and quantity of data collection methods.
- Through the inclusion of negative data when relevant to the research question or issue.
- Through an interpretive discourse to verify particular data as evidence.
- By evaluation of evidence as representative, appropriate, honest and authentic.
- By reflection and sharing our claims to knowledge.

Reflection is integral to making claims for knowledge. The 'truth' of any situation is notoriously slippery to grasp. We are distracted by unusual or exciting evidence or events, or by the weight of data from high status contributors. We must be alert to the teacher researcher's effects on the situation when collecting and interpreting data. We must also be careful about generalizing from a small number of incidents.

Validation procedures should be outlined prior to the data collection. The teacher researcher needs to:

- focus on a research question or issue and explain its significance to them and to the educational situation;
- explain what the data collection is designed to achieve;
- situate the research within a wider research community – in its literature, previous research and debate;
- keep a log or journal detailing the means of data collection, the procedural code or rules, decisions made about the use of data, the means of interpreting the data and initial conclusions that emerge;

- record the sequence of research events from initial data collection to the possible revision of the issue, implications of data interpretation and its problematizing, decisions about ceasing data collection, concluding the study and report writing;
- reflect on personal incidents and the emotional climate of the research process.

For a reader of the research report to assess its success, genuineness, honesty and, above all, truthfulness, the evidence should be easily accessible. Appendices should contain primary data, interpretation of data and relevant evidence of the procedural rules followed. In practitioner research the explanation of 'how' decisions regarding data are reached and how conclusions are confirmed is often overlooked. Yet this information is essential to an outsider or to anyone not directly involved in the research study.

Fieldnotes

Fieldnotes are the teacher researcher's record of what has been observed, and will include description of the context, locality, participants, what has taken place and what has been said. Fieldnotes made *in situ* are more reliable evidence than fieldnotes that are written up later. Fieldnotes should be as factual as possible and recorded separately from researchers' memos, which comment on and interpret the events. Fieldnotes should try to record as accurately as possible the actual language and words used by participants because individuals are differently defined through language expression. Fieldnotes should represent a thick description (Geertz 1973) of the situation, which may include maps and diagrams of participants' location and movements. It may include description of the decor, heating, participants' clothing and their relative position to each other sitting or standing. Fieldnotes are particularly useful to complement audio recording, to set the scene and to indicate non-verbal interaction. In fieldwork time needs to be set aside for writing memos *in situ*, or as soon as possible later, as well as time for data interpretation.

Triangulation

Triangulation is a technique for studying a situation from multiple perspectives; for example using the pupil, the teacher and the teacher researcher provides three perspectives. Yet multiple perspectives can be applied by including the observations of a collaborating outsider, a headteacher, an educational psychologist, an LEA officer or parents (see Elliott 1991; Altrichter *et al.* 1993). A specific lesson may be recorded and observed from different positions, and those concerned discuss their data and its meaning with each other. A record of the agreements and/or conflicts that arise in the discussion will indicate whether further investigation is necessary or whether a consensus can be agreed. Different perspectives provide the opportunity to detect bias through divergent or contradictory data. If divergence is minimal then validation is assured, whereas if it is noticeably divergent further investigation may be required. Triangulating the data strengthens its validation. It helps to overcome the distortion of one researcher's perception. For example, if the teacher's interview corroborates the observer's account of an event, or lesson, then the greater is the teacher researcher's confidence in the reliability of data.

Triangulation of research methods is also necessary to overcome an overdependence on talk by bringing in written resources and other data collection methods. Different sources of data provide a wider means of verification. For example, in a chosen lesson, a video camera may be used to record the events, a pupil may be interviewed about his or her experiences of the lesson and the teacher may provide lesson notes and documentation to back up his or her plans and intentions for the lesson. In addition, a colleague or observer may take notes of the sequence and nature of events as they unfold. Therefore, after the lesson is over, there will be four methods of data collection to be interpreted from at least four different perspectives. Data can be collected from different groups at one point in time or from the same group at different times.

Triangulation can also apply to the interpretation of the data. When the data is being interpreted, it may be coded into clusters and themes to provide a framework for understanding the problematics of the situation. This may be undertaken solely by the teacher researcher. Alternatively, it could be interpreted by a group of research participants not associated with the specific lesson used for investigation, in addition to the interpretation by the direct participants. At least three different interpretations could be made of the data collected. The process evolves in interaction with the data collection process *in situ* as the investigation progresses. When data is triangulated it offers an excellent basis for dialogue between people in different roles, opening out understanding and providing a means to resolve practical concerns and conflicts. Several levels of interpretation of the evidence, e.g. on the individual, group, institutional or societal level, are advocated (Denzin 1978). Educational contexts are ideal settings for triangulation because of their complex and intricate nature.

Case study

This is the study of complex educational events in their natural context. Circumstances are studied as they unfold, and every aspect of the specific context is equally considered to be significant. Case study is not simply the study of a single person, group or situation. It is used to illustrate, describe or evaluate a specific period of time, a context, a set of events, a process or a programme.

A case study of an individual pupil should be sensitively considered. The teacher researcher may be in danger of 'singling out' pupils for special investigation, thus in a sense increasing their segregation from peers. The problem may be overcome by collecting data when the pupil is in a group or using the same investigative techniques with more than one pupil, so that single targeting is avoided.

Case studies are often used to broaden or illuminate an established category or issue, e.g. to redefine the theoretical classification of disaffection. When case studies are written in the first person they are usually referred to as case reports, whereas case studies are third person reports, where other persons are the focus of the story. The best case studies have a plot and some dramatic tension. They are located; they reveal motives, agency and intention and reflect the social and cultural contexts within which they occur (Schulman 1992).

The case study can also demonstrate the hermeneutic circle, where description is a means of achieving interpretation through understanding. To be correct, interpretation needs to be protected against irrelevant ideas and the limitations imposed; it concentrates thought and focuses on what is relevant. It is important in all research to be aware of one's own views so that the situation under investigation presents itself in all its originality, and therefore is able to assert its own truth against one's own long-held beliefs. The critical question of hermeneutics is to distinguish the true prejudices, by which we understand, from the false ones, by which we misunderstand. As long as we are influenced by prejudice we do not know how to make balanced judgements. Understanding begins when something requires a fundamental suspension of our prejudices. All suspension of judgement and prejudice leads to the formation of questions that can open up different possibilities. Understanding is achieved by placing oneself within a process of tradition, where past and present are constantly fused. We produce tradition ourselves by understanding and participating in its evolution and hence determine it ourselves. The circular relationship of understanding the whole in terms of the detail, and the detail in terms of the whole, is the principle of modern hermeneutics (Gadamer 1981: 236). Understanding is constantly moving from the whole to the part and back to the whole. Our task is to extend in concentric circles and to unify the understanding and meaning. The harmony of all the details with the whole is the criterion for correct understanding.

Focus groups

Focus groups can operate independently as a means of collecting and interpreting data, or they can complement both quantitative and qualitative methods. The distinguishing feature of focus groups is their use of group interaction to discuss data, produce data and provide insights that would not be available in single interview situations. Focus groups are usually created and managed by the lead or main teacher researcher. Because they are not based on natural settings, groups may not be chosen as a primary source of data if natural settings can provide similar data through participant observation. Although the focus group can provide data with minimal direct researcher input, the researcher has less control of the data collection process in comparison to a single interview. Many research studies begin with data from focus groups, in which topics of interest to the teacher researcher are discussed. This helps the teacher researcher to consider the issues within a wide range of opinion and experience brought to the group by its members, who may include students. The research's initial direction, methods and interpretation may be influenced by the focus group data.

Focus groups normally contain between six and fifteen members. A number of focus groups may be required for a research study. A single group may fail to run, and multiple groups will overcome this problem. However, a minimum number of focus groups carefully chosen for their specific membership and their location may be necessary, but can create off-site problems related to travel, cost and time.

The group always influences its members' responses through the dynamics of the interaction. If the research topic or issue is very controversial, some members may speak more confidently than others. Careful observation and management of the group may, in this case, point to the need for supplementary individual interviews to ensure that members feel free to express their views.

Interviews

An interview is a verbal exchange between the teacher researcher and another participant or group of participants. It is a direct and flexible form of interaction. It can elicit information. The interviewer can pursue responses on the spot, request elaboration or redefinition of a response and probe attitudes or feelings at greater depth than using other research techniques. The interviewer can also diffuse tense or nervous interview situations by unfocusing from the topic or using humour.

A good interviewer creates a climate of rapport and trust, says as little as possible to elicit responses and controls their own personal bias. They need to focus 100 per cent on the interviewee and the task in hand, in as neutral a manner as possible, rising above unpleasant locational factors (like odours), interruptions, distraction and deflection. As with questionnaires, it is best to begin the interview with factual questions about the interviewee. Personal or controversial questions are best left until later in the interview, although an experienced interviewer will judge the best time for such questions as the opportunity arises.

There are different kinds of interview: formal and structured, and informal and unstructured. The formal/structured interview is planned in advance. Questions are written and sequenced in a logical order and the interviewer or interviewee has little freedom for modifications. It provides a closed situation in comparison to the informal/unstructured interview. The informal interview is conducted with minimal control. The interviewee is encouraged to express his or her responses as freely and fully as he or she chooses. An informal interview still requires careful planning to ensure the establishment of rapport from the outset, which is necessary to elicit the best results. Interviewer guidance and control are minimal except to focus the responses on the topic as far as possible. Deviations can be tolerated if judged relevant; otherwise a subtle intervention to refocus will be required. Informal interviewing suits complex situations where the interviewee's knowledge is limited. Techniques in this situation include repeating interviewees' responses as the interviewer understands them, elucidating unclear responses and probing for deeper disclosure. The interviewee would be expected to talk for 80–90 per cent of the interview time.

All interviews should be recorded using an audio recorder or written notes. Open interviews in particular will be difficult to record *in situ* without electronic support, whereas in formal interviews a response sheet or inventory can be prepared in advance. All interviewees should be asked for their permission to record, and written notes can replace the tape recorder if its use is refused. Interviewees should be selected because of their specific role, status or experience in relation to the research questions identified.

However, if interviews are taped they will need to be transcribed, noting both direct answers and interactional para-language. An entire tape may need to be played more than once to understand more clearly the interviewees' perspective on the topic. The actual language used should be recorded as 'primary' data. Key words and phrases, repeated comments and perspectives should be coded and noted. Then it is possible to tabulate repeated phrases and comments numerically and also to bank them in relation to their relevance and meaning. The transcripts can throw up data with similar meanings, which can lead to the discovery of common themes that unite clusters into more general research categories.

A summary of each individual interview can be made in this way using coding, clustering and themes and categories. All the interviews can be summarized in an identical manner and compared for variation or for a common thematic consensus. The emerging themes or contradictions can then be related back to the original research question or issue, recognizing the context and relevance of their discovery.

A piloting of interview schedules, or questions planned to conduct 'open' interviews, should take place in a replicated context with the interviewer. Controls and safeguards against bias in the data should be identified, e.g. were leading questions used, was emotional tone used to elicit certain responses, or were questions linguistically slanted to ensure a specific response?

The interviewer's gender, appearance, race, religion or language facility may influence the interviewee's responses. These factors should be noted and reviewed as relevant or otherwise. Their nature and significance can be evaluated via a pilot study.

For the research to meet ethical standards, interviewees need to be primed in advance about the general questions they are expected to answer, the interview location, its length and the participants named. More than two people may be present – there may be two interviewees, two interviewers or an observer in support of the interviewer or interviewee. Interviewees should be given an outline of questions to be posed in advance of the interview to enable them to feel confident about what exactly is to take place and what is expected of them.

Telephone interviews may be necessary when a chosen sample are at a distance. Interview costs exclude the cost of interviewer travel and opportunities arise for broader geographic accessibility. Telephone interviews can be easily monitored, recorded and checked for auditing purposes. Busy people may prefer this kind of interview, as it is economical with time. Personal dangers to interviewers are also diminished, but there may be the disadvantage of not being able to interview respondents with no access to a telephone, e.g. children, young people or the economically disadvantaged. The problem about the interviewee being influenced by gender, appearance etc. is less relevant.

In conclusion, an interviewer should:

- develop a detailed interview schedule and a means of its interpretation in advance;
- pilot the interview schedule and practise interview skills;
- ensure that leading or biased questions are absent;
- ask questions related to the interviewee's background and experience in a language they understand.

Questionnaires

A questionnaire is an economical method of collecting data. It will reach more people and take up less time than an interview. When planning the use of a questionnaire, its appropriateness in the specific research study needs to be considered in relation to the following questions.

- What specific information will the questionnaire gather that another research method would not?
- What aspect of your research question or issue do you wish to investigate?

You will need to explain the purpose of your study in a short covering letter. Attention in questionnaire construction needs to be paid to the language used, the order of questions and the format of the questionnaire. The opening questions set the scene for respondents, attract their attention and should reduce anxiety. Screening questions are best at the beginning, e.g. 'Do you enjoy your work with children with SEN?' Sensitive questions are best left to the latter half or the end of the questionnaire. For example, early questions about teaching children with SEN should set the scene so that questions about possible problems or ideas for improvement are left until later. Arrows can be used to direct respondents to later questions when intervening questions are irrelevant. Broad questions set the scene, while specific detailed questions build on them by expanding their detail. Before the questionnaire is administered it should be piloted. Similar persons or groups should be found to trial the questionnaire. Their interpretation of the questions, their reactions and responses, will either confirm or disconfirm your original intentions for the questionnaire. The piloting of a questionnaire is essential to avoid possible confusion or ambiguity, which would be irritating for both respondents and teacher researcher. Make sure that the respondents are given the opportunity to write comments about possible improvement of the questionnaire. Their responses should also allow you to determine whether the methods you have planned to summarize and interpret the data will work satisfactorily. Additional questions may be suggested in cases where disagreement is found to the response to a particular question. The construction of additional questions will clear up any misunderstanding and avoid frustration.

The target group must be identified before the questionnaire is constructed, because this may influence its language and format. Children and young people may be supported in answering a questionnaire if questions are read for them, individually or in a group, and their answers recorded on a prepared response schedule. When you have decided what you need to know and who could provide this information, a preliminary questionnaire can be drawn up. Questions may be 'open' or 'closed'. Closed questions permit only certain set responses, like a multiple choice question. Open questions invite the respondents to write what they wish. Points to remember are:

- use language that will be easily understood by the target group;
- ensure that the questionnaire and its questions are short and simple;
- make the format attractive;
- organize and lay out questions in a clear, easy to follow manner;
- organize the questionnaire in a logical sequence, using transitional tactics when changing the focus of questions;
- avoid asking biased or leading questions;
- avoid asking negative questions;
- ask a general question to set the scene for specific questions;
- if you need to investigate negative aspects of a situation, ask a positive question before a negative one (e.g. 'What do you like about . . .?' 'What do you dislike about . . .?');
- with multiple choice questions, make sure your known alternatives are listed, but always include 'other' for the respondents to specify for themselves and/or 'none of the above'.

A recurring problem with questionnaires is their low response rate. Yet refusers may be critical to the balance of the sample. If questionnaires are numbered or identified in some way, respondents can be checked in relation to crucial variables like age, experience, role or status. They may be approached again and persuaded to provide information by another method, e.g. a telephone interview, if this is essential to the research. Respondents can be offered small rewards for completing and returning the questionnaire.

Covering letter

The covering letter should be professional, brief and encouraging. It should outline a good argument for the return of the questionnaire and assure confidentiality. The aims of the research should be briefly explained, as well as its possible use, including accessibility to the completed research report. To have the letter signed by a person of high status will lend it added weight, e.g. a signature may be obtained from the chairperson of the faculty research committee or an LEA chief education officer. These persons may also be useful in the dissemination and publication of the finished research report.

The questionnaire return date should be set at less than two weeks and more than one. Urgency in the response works better than a delayed date, where the questionnaire may be put aside and forgotten. It may be opportune to use specific venues, e.g. school meetings, conferences or courses where the target group are present and where respondents can answer on the spot. In these cases, a total sample might be obtained without postal costs or missed deadline returns. The presentation and format of the questionnaire will also determine how it is perceived and whether or not it will be returned.

Interpretation of questionnaires

The questionnaire should be precoded before its release. Some simple interpretations to be noted in advance are:

- differentiation between factual and interpretive questions;
- the creation of tables or charts for the data;
- the creation of a coding framework for the data;
- the use of coding for the interpretive questions, e.g. using key words and phrases, positive/negative attitude or expected/unexpected responses;
- variables in the data can be cross-tabulated using percentages, which are clearly self-explanatory;
- statistical sources can take interpretation further by measuring variables and the value of their relationships to each other.

Life history and biography

Biographies or accounts of people's lives are increasing being used in teacher research as a means of understanding classroom practice and behaviour (Goodson 1992). The images that teachers have of themselves influence how they cope in the classroom and how they are professionally socialized. The stories of people's life experiences or histories unfold differentially in relation to the situation and the audience. Life is not one story or history but many overlapping narratives. Memory alters the perception of events over time and many vignettes may form a more composite whole. Therefore, the role of the teacher researcher in biography is to elicit biographical stories that will integrate the cultural, social, public and private aspects of lives (Sikes 1997; Goodson 2001). Life history has seen a resurgence in postmodern culture because it can confidently represent the multiple and partial nature of human life (Munro 1998). However, all life histories are an interpretation of the reality of lived experiences, and are therefore subjectively coloured. A selective and personal commentary is presented for biographical research. It is then the teacher researcher's role to interpret the words and language used in interviews and written texts to reshape the texts for another audience. Goodson (2001) suggests that there are two interpretive layers, in the movement from life story to life history. In the former, the informant relates his or her life story; in the latter, life history is constructed through a new range of interviews and documentary data. Goodson warns that ethical issues are dominant in this movement, involving issues of process and power.

It is the teacher researcher's role to choose informants, set up biographical interviews and record, transcribe and interpret the stories told. Multiple methods for triangulating the data may be used as and when appropriate to confirm accounts, but interpretation of free-standing accounts can be validated by their nature and intention.

Shadow study

A shadow study is a research technique to enable the teacher researcher to experience the everyday world of key participants beyond their immediate location. It may, however, be a collaborating outsider who undertakes the 'shadowing'. The purpose of 'shadowing' is to gain insider information about the role and experiences of a colleague, teacher, headteacher or pupil. Because the teacher researcher is not in his or her normal role he or she becomes a participant observer taking fieldnotes and recording the daily activities of the chosen participant. A shadow study is just what the word shadow implies. The teacher researcher tries to remain as 'invisible' as possible when vicariously experiencing someone else's life. The use of a small handheld video might support the process, but technology that is too intrusive may put others involved with the chosen participant on their guard. Advance warning of the plan may need to be conveyed to peripheral as well as key participants. It is an effective research technique when the data to be collected is anticipated in advance, so as to support the planning of evidence gathering procedures and interpretive strategies. However, consideration must be given to the circumstances of the study and the appropriateness or otherwise of the teacher researcher proceeding in certain high-risk or private situations.

Permission must be sought from the 'shadowed' person or from teachers, parents or guardians in the case of a minor. In a shadow study it isn't necessary to record everything, only those things considered relevant to the research. A sequence of events should be described at timed intervals. The context and locality should be noted, as well as personal comments about what is taking place. A prepared format can provide a framework for the observations. For example:

Time/context	Behaviour/activities of 'shadowed'	Comments/personal impressions

A plan for the selection of specific times for the shadowing will overcome indecision on the spot, e.g. should shadowing include lunch and breaks? These decisions influence the kind of evidence recorded and its interpretation. Professional decision-making is made more transparent through notes on why different recording techniques are used, or changed *in situ* to suit the reality.

A shadow study is often supplemented by an interview with the 'shadowed' to confirm assumptions made or to verify personal perceptions and impressions. A controversial incident may occur during the shadow study, and the 'shadowed' may need to discuss it and the observer's interpretation of it. The 'shadowed' may feel the need to explain motives and intentions to the teacher researcher. The teacher researcher must allow for any such events and respect the 'shadowed' person's right to know how their behaviour is to be publicly represented.

Evaluation

Action research is a form of professional evaluation, because the value of the investigation lies in its application and utilization. The process of consistent and constant evaluation may be more important than the eventual outcomes of the research. The provision of evidence and arguments to support the validity of the evidence provide a basis for informed action. The fact that the action research takes place through a democratic and inclusive process confers ownership of the decisions and their outcomes on participants, thus weakening extreme recommendations or action to achieve of unrealistic goals. Therefore, the action research process uses evidence for possible change and ensures that participants in the study learn self-evaluation via the demonstration of reflective educational practice.

Whole-school evaluation may depend on systems of evaluation, such as internal school appraisal and external school inspections, that view staff development as separate from teacher evaluation (Duke 1995). But teacher and professional evaluation systems that are formative use self-evaluation as the core of the process. Teacher self-evaluation provokes teachers to review and critique their own professional activities, values and influence for the purpose of better educational practices. The teacher researcher decides what criteria are best to judge his or her values, attitudes, activities and influence. He or she decides on the methods to be used to evaluate professional practices. The concept of self-evaluation is associated with the reflective practitioner, reflection in and on practice, educational action research and teacher connoisseurship (Eisner 1976). These approaches direct teacher researchers to assessment of their own practice, with the aim of bettering and changing unsatisfactory situations. It is formative in the sense that action is taken to change the situation based on empirical evidence. It strengthens educational practice associated with specific goals like inclusion.

Sampling

All empirical research is concerned with sampling. These procedures can be classified as opportunity sampling, representative sampling and random sampling (Brown and Dowling 1998).

Opportunity sampling uses friends, colleagues and research participants within one's professional ambit. These contacts can refer the researcher to a wider network of participants, causing a snowball effect.

Representative sampling involves locating participants within a particular category, e.g. boys with Down's syndrome. Therefore, the chosen sample can be taken to be representative of the group as a whole because of their background, location or other factors. A quota sample is a development of the representative sample because the quota will refine the representative group in terms of, for example, age or educational placement and will select equal representation within each category.

Random sampling has a very precise meaning in statistical analysis. It means that each person has an equal possibility of being selected. The sampling may be necessary, e.g. when investigating the experiences of special school pupils in a local authority. A list of pupils attending special schools can be made up from the LEA and other databases, from which a random sample is drawn. There is an endless combination of numerical possibilities that can be called upon, depending on the number of pupils to be included. It can be calculated as every tenth name, or selected as take two, miss two and so on. In statistical analysis the theory of probability can be utilized, particularly when considering large numbers. Sampling may be a technique chosen initially in the action research process to locate participants and define the boundaries of the research. It is a useful tool for selecting participants in a locality for interviews, for questionnaires or for observation.

Use of statistics

The use of statistical methods in action research can help in data collection and provides a useful tool for sorting out numerical evidence. Quantitative or numerical evidence may be used when choosing participants, e.g. when a LEA officer wishes to select a group of headteachers to investigate their professional problems related to inclusive practice and thus find a better means of supporting them. A sampling procedure could be used to define a group for more in-depth investigation through, for example, the use of focus groups.

Basic statistical knowledge is also required for the interpretation and comparison of individual student test scores. Various methods are available for measuring the relative value of a score, e.g. the use of percentiles. Many standardized tests for children and young people with SEN use variables to which numbers or values are assigned. Once values are assigned they can be measured, and are referred to as parameters.

Initially the teacher researcher may use descriptive statistics to organize, summarize or describe the measures of a sample. For example, the extent of a classroom reading problem can be measured with a standardized test using 'reading ages'. A teacher using action research may wish to improve the reading ability of her students. She begins by appraising the situation using standardized tests. She records the results on a histogram, graph or pie chart. She then selects a sample of students for her enrichment programme. She plans to use self-evaluation of her teaching, and verbal feedback from students, colleagues and parents. Finally, she may confirm her success or otherwise by reusing the same standardized test to check progress on a technical level. However, she also develops a deeper understanding of how her students learn, their motivation, their learning styles and her skills and expertise by using supplementary data collection methods in the process. Her decision to continue with a specific reading enrichment programme will depend on much more than simply the 'test' scores.

Other methods

Other research methods include document investigation, using historical resources, professional and school archives, the Internet, minutes of meetings, student profiles and statements. All relevant sources of evidence that will inform the teacher researcher from the beginning should be reviewed and evaluated on their merit. Ask yourself what must be reviewed and what will provide a useful platform for the launch of the study.

For example, discourse analysis examines accounts as they occur in the situation, and is a useful means of illustrating the complexity of everyday conversations (see Coulthard 1985; Potter and Wetherall 1987). It uses specific techniques to investigate why things are created as they are through speech, and seeks to explain their verbal construction. Ethogenic research (Harré 1978) considers intentions, behaviour and the person's understanding of the social rules governing their behaviour. This method adopts a common sense approach to understanding the social world, and sources of evidence are drawn from wherever possible to illustrate the meaning of behaviour in edu-cational contexts. The advantage of ethogenic research is the provision of insights through the interpretation of accounts of social episodes (Cohen and Manion 1989). Social events are described in relation to gestures, speech, feel-ings and intentions, and may be drawn from past or present events or future intentions. The authenticity of accounts can be corroborated by triangulation of multiple perspectives, data collection and interpretation.

The above methods can be employed by participants in the Research to support and triangulate 'insider' evidence.

CHAPTER SEVEN

The ethics of practitioner research

Regardless of the methodological positions we take and the substantive interests that direct our work, all who work in the social sciences and education deal in the moral dimension of their practice. Doing research involves emotions like hope, attentiveness and caring, which lie outside of the technological and scientific mind set of educational culture. Difference is eliminated in classrooms, where the pretence of technical equality erases living differences, wiping away distinctions such as colour and ability narrowly defined, but also needs, interest, emotions, cultural and ethnic variety and world view (Elbaz 1991). The homogenization, the simplistic belief in certainty and the emotional flattening that technological progress brings with it need serious questioning.

Teaching as a professional activity is based on theoretical knowledge and research. Teacher researchers as professionals are primarily committed to the well-being of their pupils. To ensure that teachers always act in their pupils' interests, they also reserve the right to make autonomous judgements free from external constraints, except where professional policies and procedures are accepted. They can make decisions about the course of action they consider best in different situations. A teacher researcher's professional concern for their pupils extends their responsibility beyond the school to parents, the local community, employers and government. This may lead to tensions and contradictions with wider interests when teachers prioritize the educational interests of their pupils. This situation requires an ethical awareness of the practice of education to help to decide the best course of action when the existing social order frustrates progress for inclusion. The awareness develops from practice grounded in educational theory and research. The theory is practical in the sense that it is determined in the ways it relates to practice.

Carr (1987) asserts that practice is only educational when it occurs in a wider ethical awareness. In his words, 'The educational character of any practice can only be made intelligible by reference to an ethical disposition to proceed

according to some more or less tacit understanding of what it is to act educationally' (Carr 1987: 166). This suggests that an educational act, like direct
support for inclusive forms of practice, is informed on a moral or ethical
level. If inclusive practice is unreflective and lacks a moral awareness, it is
action without an educational purpose. What does this mean if we apply
this argument to research for inclusion? The research may be based on an
educational idea about inclusion, but it will not be intelligible unless, or until,
it is situated in a moral awareness or reflexivity about 'how to' realize the
educational purpose of inclusion in a practical context. The ideas and theories
that teacher researchers already hold will operate to inform action for the
research participants and for readers of the research record. Failure to reflect on
existing theories and ideas will make the written research record interesting,
but futile, reading, because without a relationship to the tangible reality of
educational contexts, which indicates what action could, should or has to be
taken, it has no ethical significance. It is in action that inclusive practice is
represented and changed.

Good research should also model forms of social action that are democratic
and inclusive in their development, because the democratic control of
educational enquiry is essential for communities to shape their futures.
Respecting everyone who participates in the research, being receptive to each
other's concerns through the free and honest communication of ideas and
proposed actions, demands a discourse that aims to model free expression
and equitable participation and trust, i.e. democratic operating principles.
However, such discourse does not guarantee that consensus will always
occur. Tensions and conflict are inevitable. Consequently, every good research
project involving active participation in professional practice depends on the
establishment of a workable code of ethics from the start.

All engagement in, or with, research in schools, or educational institutions,
raises issues of trust in relationships. Questions arise. How will an observer in
a classroom use the information gathered about the teaching? With whom
will the information be shared? Can an interviewer be trusted to interview
pupils in a manner that is non-manipulative and fair? If evidence of teaching
problems is shared with others, will some teachers be unfairly judged as
problem teachers? Collaborative school- and classroom-based research, carried
out with colleagues, university tutors or researchers, that engages others in
discussion about its practical implications for inclusive practice requires
access to potentially sensitive data that is traditionally regarded as 'private'
to individual teachers. Releasing it to a more public audience has implications
for those teachers or pupils who provide the evidence in the first place. It is
important that the research process be carried out in an ethically defensive
manner, to protect individual teachers and pupils from possible misuses of
data, and to decrease threat in the research process. Establishing an agreed
code of practice governing the conditions under which data is gathered, released
and used is essential from the start. A draft code helps to secure trust in those
involved and ensures the ethical defensibility of school-based collaborative
research. Establishing trusting relationships between research participants
depends on more than just goodwill and oral agreements. A written code

provides the opportunity for participants to accept the rules of procedure or to withdraw from the action. Trusting relationships are the foundation for deconstruction, i.e. uncovering issues and problems with openness and honesty, and encouraging everyone involved to take action to improve matters.

The following draft code provides a useful working example and has been adapted from an original research code of practice used in the Norwich Area Schools Consortium (NASC) project at CARE, University of East Anglia. It sets out basic principles about what procedures are expected to occur when teachers and pupils are involved in observations and interviewing.

Classroom observations and interviews involving teachers and pupil

1 Teacher and school permission should be obtained in advance for opportunities to observe lessons and interview teachers and pupils.
2 The methods and focus of the observations and interviews should be negotiated with the school and teachers, and agreed in advance of lessons.
3 When children or young people are involved in observation or interviews, they or their parents or carers should be informed and permission sought about the nature of the data collected and the extent of its release to the public.
4 Teachers should have access to all observational and interview records that concern them.
5 Pupils should be informed prior to interviews and observations that the data may be accessed by teachers and others, and their permission should be sought about wider access before gathering the data.
6 Teachers should have access to observations and interviews with pupils on condition that pupils' permission has been obtained for the release of the data.
7 Immediately following any interview, the interviewee should be given the opportunity to qualify anything they have said, to amend or add to it, or even strike it off the record.
8 All observational and interview records should remain confidential between participants until their use for purposes of reporting to, or sharing with, others is agreed.
9 When pupils are interviewed by their teachers they should be given the same guarantees as stated in points 7 and 8.
10 Video recordings, audio tapes and photographs should also be negotiated and agreed by participants before sharing or publication beyond the classroom or school concerned.

The research may extend beyond the 'insider's' school to include investigation in a wider school context.

Access to and release of data by outside researchers in schools

1 The focus of the research should be agreed by the school(s) concerned.
2 Information about the aims of the research and its methodology should be made available to all school staff, with opportunities for them to discuss it with the researcher.
3 The researcher should not assume automatic rights to observe all or any events and situations in the school without advance permission from those involved.
4 Teachers and pupils have the right, without prejudice, to refuse requests for interviews, video recordings, audio recordings or photographs.
5 Whenever possible advance notice should be given by the researcher about the focus and manner of the data collection.
6 No observational, interview or other data will be included in research reports, or be made accessible to others in any form, without the permission of those individuals or groups who provided it or allowed access to it.
7 Anonymity should be guaranteed to individuals whose actions and views are evidenced in research reports. Where anonymity is clearly not sufficient to hide the identity of participants, the recording of relevant actions and views should be negotiated and agreed between the researcher and those concerned.
8 Anonymity should be guaranteed to individuals in schools and LEAs unless they request otherwise.
9 Before research reports are made public beyond the participants, a draft should be circulated to or shared with participants for comments, discussion and feedback.
10 Where there is disagreement, comment and discussion of relevant sections of draft reports should be included in the final drafts to the satisfaction of pupils, teachers, schools and LEAs.
11 Any disagreements related to representation or interpretation of evidence should be indicated, and decisions about their resolution explained in the final draft.

Regardless of the research focus or whether it is an insider or outsider doing the research, certain principles for research procedure in schools (like those above) can be generalized for all teacher researchers. The negotiation and agreement of a code of practice informs all research participants, whether insider or outsider, about their rights and obligations. It anticipates possible problems with ownership, responsibilities and individual rights. It provides an informal agreement about research procedures and their consequences. It avoids the many pitfalls that are likely to occur in the process of educational investigations for inclusive practice.

Discussion of the proposed research with the headteacher, and anyone else involved within the school or LEA, with professionals outside the school and with parents and pupils is imperative from the outset.

The success of action research as a means of increasing inclusive practice depends upon negotiating the engagement of teachers and others with research in schools, LEAs and with health and social services providers. Engagement in research may involve teachers collaborating together in the gathering, sharing and interpretation of data from other schools and classrooms. It may involve staff in local schools or professional agencies in, for example, the investigation of inclusive practice in a LEA. Teacher researchers' engagement in research may also involve collaborating with professional researchers in data collection, interpretation and reporting the findings and evidence to others. This raises issues about forming trusting relationships in research practice that will influence its scope and quality. It is an interactive process within which change is occurring through the research process itself. Attitudes and practices may be changed during the development of the research without full awareness of its happening and no specific focus on, or recording of, this aspect of the process. Yet to understand fully how research changes practice, changes in values and attitudes must be given further attention (see Chapter 8).

Vulnerable research participants

It may be important to use sensitive research methods for the investigation of inclusive practice. Many of the participants in the research could be seen as more vulnerable and subject to manipulation in research contexts because of their educational differences and marginalized status.

The question of power relationships arises in relation to different kinds of discourses in educational research. There are profound implications for teacher researchers that arise from the post-structural focus upon persons as participants in the research process. The teacher researcher must negotiate the balance of 'voices' raised in the research process. The giving of voice to oppressed groups and the movement towards democratic and transformative research are more closely aligned to the interests and needs of these people, as expressed by themselves.

In any society there are vulnerable individuals who have little power over events that affect them or control over their own space in the world. There are also 'groups' in society that, because of their recognized attributes, have little power in social and cultural interactions. These groups are recognized in different ways by different professional alignments in society. For example, adults and young people with special needs and disabilities are recognized in health, care and educational contexts, because it is these professional groups that identify their membership, define their needs and make provision for them. Sociologists identify groups from evidence of oppression through racism, sexism, ageism and general discrimination against marginalized people in society like refugees or Travelling people. Depending on which discipline is deciding on the definition of 'vulnerability', the individuals or groups covered by the term will vary. However, for our purposes the term applies to marginalized individuals and groups in society, who are seen to have less power over their lives than naturalized, educated, employed, healthy, influential individuals or groups who live in the same community. This definition covers children and young people with different or additional learning needs, adults and groups with diminished roles and rights in their communities.

Yet another group that decides the categories of people they research is made up of the researchers themselves. The research process is often characterized by the exercise of power and the workings of vested interests. Yet it is the responsibility of practitioner researchers to become more reflexive and aware, to struggle against undue exercise of power by aligning their research with the interests of the less powerful rather than the more powerful. This suggests that research involving vulnerable people should prioritize participants' best interests and focus their research aims on their identified needs.

When the researchers define the category of person, e.g. 'children with SEN', they are effectively excluding the 'researched' from any participation in the construction of knowledge about themselves. The researched are then to be known in terms of the reductionist categories to which researchers allocate them.

How does one investigate inclusive practice by constructing the 'researched' in a manner that is not inherently reductionist? It is crucial that participants be offered the opportunity to construct knowledge about themselves by having their voices represented in the research process. It is also important to allow them to use, or create, identities that they accept and feel comfortable with. This requires awareness of the use of one-sided research questions, loaded in favour of a specific response.

Regardless of the different research 'methods' used with vulnerable people, it is vital that serious consideration is given to how the data is to be used. The methods, for example, may include interviews, questionnaires, video, audio or photographic recording, shadow studies, case studies and biographical narratives. In each of these methods there is a possibility of the abuse of power relationships. The initial approach by the teacher researcher to someone to take part in the research is loaded in favour of the researcher. How feasible is it for a vulnerable person or group to refuse to participate? How clearly are the aims of the research explained and understood by the persons who are to be 'researched' or to participate? How far is their commitment to the time, effort and process fully explained and understood? Has a code of practice been explained, outlining the expectations of both parties regarding the process and product of the research? Who will own the data? Who will negotiate and decide about what is published and for what audience? Are the possible repercussions on the lives of the 'research participants' fully realized and explained by the researcher?

It can be assumed that the (teacher) researcher is more powerful than the researched, so great care and sensitivity has to be employed in the development and negotiation, collection and publication of the data. Another safe assumption is that the teacher researcher may be an 'outsider' in the group being researched, because he or she is not a 'vulnerable' person. Yet teacher researchers are participants in the research process and, if the processes are reductionist and oppressive, they may be acting as oppressors, even if they try to align themselves through temporary membership of the oppressed or vulnerable group. It is questionable whether anyone who is not a member of a specific social group will fully be able to replace their own identity with that of another for the sake of the research, although they may attempt to struggle with a reconstructed self for its short life.

Much of the debate in educational research on the topic of children and adults with different learning and cultural needs centres on the issues of how 'truth' can be accessed. The question is, who is capable of uncovering the truth and proclaiming it? Some see the truth of the situation under investigation as coming from the authentic voices of people who experience segregation or marginalization in education or society. Others favour a research approach that puts the researched in the foreground, enabling their voices to be heard and giving them more control of the research process. But the question that arises from these issues is whether the authoritative teacher researcher's voice is subsequently marginalized and whether there is space left for it to operate. How can the teacher researcher make a valid claim to be facilitating a genuine process to uncover the truth if they are seen, by the participants, as the first arbiter and final editor of the research data? The answer lies partly in the deliberate construction of multiple perspectives by different participants in the research, which are developed and given voice in the research report with the aim of critiquing power relations that are oppressive or creating vulnerabilities for the participants. Seeking out alternative versions of what inclusion means in context becomes a political activity for critiquing the constructions of the 'researched', and creates possible action to transform the relationships of the groups involved. It is important to establish the bases for claims that are made to 'truth' and to determine the conditions under which people with different views can engage in debate (Habermas 1986).

Doing research with vulnerable people brings with it a set of ethical problems that are not in themselves separate from ethical issues in education generally. Ethical issues may be connected to the issues of equality and justice but may also be connected to personal relationships and communities. Research ethics have been defined in a number of publications by professional associations. For example, the British Educational Research Association (1992) has developed guidelines for educational researchers. Inherent in the many guidelines produced by learned societies (psychology, sociology etc.) is the fair treatment of vulnerable people, although it may not always be explicitly defined.

Questions have been raised about forms of research carried out previously. For example:

- offering bribes to participants;
- putting participants in physical danger;
- causing mental stress to participants;
- risking reputations and lives.

When is it permissible to offer bribes for information or actions in the cause of research? Do the research participants fully appreciate that they may be risking life or reputation, or putting additional stress on themselves, as a result of divulging certain facts or information to the researcher? Ethically, it is imperative to inform participants of the possible consequences of their actions and to negotiate the publication of such information under their real name or anonymously, depending on what they wish. In some cases it might be incumbent on the researcher to protect the researched by not revealing the 'truth' of the situation. Neither is it ethical to conceal or deceive participants by giving them deliberately false information about the aims and methods of the research.

Informed consent should be acquired for children and people who are not mentally competent in research situations. Permission from the institution or school head or the director of a hospital or psychiatric centre should be sought. If in doubt, it is important to get the consent of parents or legal guardians. Inform them of the aims of the research, and the length of time it will take overall, the questions to be asked, as well as the time and commitment expected from the participants. However, in educational research it is only possible to inform participants in general terms, with the proviso of negotiating the data interactively with participants throughout the research process, which can be covered by an agreed and negotiated code of practice.

Life history and biography

In biographical research, ethical issues figure large, because such research deals with intimate and personal material. The first ethical question that arises in biographical research is the degree of intrusiveness acceptable to both parties. Personally, I have found when doing research that people enjoy talking about themselves and can easily be coaxed or seduced to say more than they may have originally intended. A good interviewer will establish a situation of mutual trust and this may lead to a flow of information that requires sensitive handling. Sometimes matters of a confidential nature are aired during the interview and need to be 'removed' from the primary data in any form that may be threatening to the 'researched', e.g. disclosures about illegal activities or matters with criminal overtones. In my research I assured the participants that their contributions would be anonymized and treated in a confidential way. I covered up their identities while at the same time situating the data in a culturally authentic context. I was aware of the power of my role as an interviewer, and found that censorship of some of the data was imperative to protect the interviewees from possible prosecution. Perfect and complete anonymity in educational research with vulnerable people cannot be obtained, because often the context of the situation makes it clear who is involved, especially when the data are revealing or challenging. The acknowledgement of participant and institutional contributions can be listed in a foreword in the main case report without any cross-referencing to the main text. There are many tensions in dealing with confidentiality and portrayal as Burgess (1989: 206) reminds us, 'it is evident that whatever precautions are taken to protect those involved in a field study, nothing is foolproof'.

Children and vulnerable adults are often misrepresented in research because of their lack of understanding about what is taking place, especially if the data involve testing or assessment. Many children and young people fail to comprehend fully the task required of them and its implications. This is not to 'blame' the 'researched' for their lack of understanding, but to indicate that problems of communication exist between the researched and the researcher in such situations. I have witnessed some appalling travesties of justice when people of different cultures, languages and registers have attempted to communicate in a 'test' situation. Often, profound decisions about the future of the 'testee' rest on the results, which don't always take into account the broader circumstances of the testing. When strange, unfamiliar and unnatural surroundings are used, the persons being tested or 'researched' may be severely disadvantaged.

There is also the question of how observational materials are used or made public. Many participants may not be aware that they are the 'subject' of investigation. There may be photographs that do not directly identify individuals, but they can be identified by those who know them. Can direct facial views be reproduced publicly without the permission of the person concerned? When videos show a broad frame of life, e.g. in a classroom or school, and are aimed at one data focus, like one child's behaviour, can they be publicly used, even when permission for 'individual' filming has been granted? They can take in much more of the life of the classroom or school and reveal the activities of many other participants whose permission has not been sought for public viewing. Research on inclusive practice may involve children, young people and adults with significantly less power than the teacher researcher. Therefore, it is incumbent on him or her to redress the balance by involving participants in decisions about the methods of the data gathering, the research questions to be included and the nature of the final account.

In summary:

- research on inclusive practice may well involve work with vulnerable people and groups, and decisions about how to approach the participants need to be anticipated and prepared for through a framework of interaction, such as a code of practice;
- the unequal relationship between participants and practitioner researcher must be considered in advance of publication and data sensitively reported;
- observations and data with vulnerable people may include disclosures that are legally or morally reportable to authorities, which may terminate or interrupt the study;
- data that can identify participants may need to be omitted or destroyed.

Informed consent should be sought when:

- there is a possibility of personal risk for the participants;
- children or adults with different learning needs are involved;
- participants' privacy may be invaded;

- information may be potentially damaging to participants;
- self-knowledge is potentially destructive to further participation.

Problems arise in research when participants are socially or culturally unable to refuse or to negotiate the data because of incapacity, lack of freedom or lack of status.

Overall:

- confidentiality of data must be maintained so that participants or institutions cannot be identified in ways that may be harmful or invite undesirable comparisons;
- invasion of privacy is a concern when participants reveal more than they intend in interviews or discussions;
- the right of outsiders to obtain data for secondary analysis may pose a dilemma for the practitioner researcher who has promised confidentiality to participants;
- credit should be given to participants in direct proportion to their contribution to the project, regardless of their status, e.g. ensuring that participants are listed as authors if their written submissions have been included in the research report.

The main principle of democratic forms of action research is that power relationships should be considered and no undue pressure should be put on participants to be included. If they agree, then they must be fully informed of what is expected of them and how the research will affect them personally.

Persons who cannot give their consent must be approached through an advocate who has their best interests at heart. It is also important for the researcher to discuss the issues and dilemmas that arise with friends or colleagues. Having a trusted friend or colleague to share ethical concerns with, when they occur, is beneficial in any research, but particularly critical for action research involving vulnerable individuals or groups.

CHAPTER EIGHT

The reflexive inclusion of the self

Know yourself; the unexamined life is not worth living.

(Socrates 480 BC)

Definitions of action research implicitly suggest personal transformation. There is extensive description about the instrumental and technical aims of action research, but not the same recognition of its potential as personal change. Yet personal transformation is intrinsic to the basic propositions of action research. Definitions of action research suggest personal 'transformation' through the use of a practical methodology for educational innovation, yet there can be no innovation without the ideas and plans of the innovator (O'Hanlon 1988).

Action research also claims to 'empower' the researcher in the process of improvement (Kincheloe 1991). Friere (1990) contends that in this kind of inquiry the inquirers are educating and being educated along with their students (either teachers or professionals), and that collaborative educational research is a form of consciousness-raising and a transformative pedagogical technique. Transformation is a personal process of change and redirection. It involves the person in a kind of gradual transition away from unreflective routine activity. There are numerous references in action research texts to the 'self' in terms such as self-evaluation, self-reflection and self-understanding (Carr and Kemmis 1986; Elliott 1989). The self is present in the 'investigation of a practitioner's world', which is the aim of action research (Hustler 1986; Nixon 1987). The individual is investigating an issue or concern with a personal focus (Stenhouse 1975; Elliott 1981).

It is clear that adults who use action research as a means of academic and professional development bring their own personal values and agendas to the process. For example, many professionals have deeply held religious values, which guide the direction of their personal lives and influence their professional practice. Assumptions are often made that, because teachers all believe in the value of schooling and education, they also hold the same educational values and attitudes. This is far from the truth. They naturally hold a range of values analogous with the multicultured and cultural communities from which they come, or in which they live.

A person's sense of self is influenced by professional activities, and vice versa. They are difficult to disentangle without personal self-awareness and understanding. It is difficult for teacher researchers to be transformed in the professional role without actually looking at themselves through their personal relationship to that role. It is difficult to separate personal attitudes, values and ideas like inclusion, which drive professional practice based on educational theories, and are often assumed to form the rationale for action. Yet, on closer examination, it is not always the case that established educational theories lead the way. It is likely to be personally held views about life, bias and attitudes, traumatic events and experiences that direct our actions and responses on many occasions in classrooms and schools. Learned educational theories perpetuated through professional training may represent specific methodologies, but they don't differentiate between the people who apply them. The application of educational theories that are merely conceptual may validate one intellectual perspective, but it will not necessarily succeed as a basis for positive change in any or all educational contexts. The reflective process in teacher research allows participants to differentiate between what they believe education to be about, what pupils need to know and how they meet these needs in reality. Reflection allows them to evaluate their actions in retrospect and judge whether they were right, productive, constructive or worthwhile. Teaching is an ethical activity that involves different judgements, particularly for specific ideals like inclusive practice – it is not the same for everyone.

There is a relationship between the realization of personal knowledge and the empowerment of the person. Self-understanding deepens when professional actions are articulated and defended with colleagues and research participants. The defence and explanation of practice develops a deeper understanding of one's action, particularly in situations where research evidence is shared. The sharing of professional practice increases teacher researchers' understanding of themselves and creates opportunities for them to identify personal beliefs, values and characteristics. 'Bias' in the activities, e.g. attending more to one pupil than others, once recognized, can be acknowledged and accepted. Whether or not this practice should be reduced or changed is an ethical challenge questioned through discourse and debate during the research process. There are other reasons, connected with personal attributes, that enable the research to succeed.

> Learning involves . . . at least three factors; knowledge, skill and character. Each of these must be studied. It requires judgement and art to select from the total circumstances of a case . . . It requires candour and sincerity to keep track of failures as well as success . . . It requires trained and acute observation to note the indicators of progress in learning and even more to detect their causes.
>
> (Dewey 1974)

Whether or not professional educational transformation takes place depends on the disposition and the experience of the person. If you fail in what you expected to achieve in action research, it is important to reflect on the process and acknowledge why you failed. Learning from it and capitalizing on it brings a deeper awareness of the situation and of your agency within it.

Dewey refers to the observation of learning both in others and in oneself. To gauge one's own success and progress requires critical reflection and self-evaluation. The nature of learning, its assessment and rationale are complex. Teacher researchers are encouraged to evaluate their own progress and how their success has been facilitated. Self-assessment of adult learning is an exercise in deconstructing what matters in one's own educational development. The personal characteristics of teacher researchers are known by themselves. The characteristics of artistry and judgement can be applied in the investigation when attending to the subtleties of practice. They are taken for granted in everyday activities but are crucial to the successful negotiation of change with research participants.

Although teacher researchers realize their aims by focusing on changing their practice in line with their own inclusive aims and ideals, they need to ask themselves how they form these aims. How do they know they are right? Teacher researchers need to collect evidence about the extent to which the practice is consistent with their aims for inclusive practice.

Regardless of their training, teachers somehow know intuitively how to teach and survive in a myriad of school contexts. When they are given the opportunity to examine their practices, they see the inconsistencies between what they are trying to do and what is really happening. This is when they have to reframe and problematize the principles, ideas and theories that they believe are guiding their practices. Through this restructuring, they can generate and test new forms of inclusive action and they can reconsider their own theories about practice.

They need to reconcile these theories to fit with their own character, personality, values and professional situations. An understanding of what is really happening in classrooms and schools reveals the gap between the rhetoric and the reality in inclusive practice. There are many writers who develop theoretical aspects of abstract ideals like democracy, equality, social justice, and inclusion, yet in real everyday practice they act differently from their own advocacy. They do this because they have little or no self-knowledge or understanding. They don't understand themselves as agents of change or as actors in educational contexts. They have not had the opportunity to research their own practice or receive critical or constructive feedback about it. So they continue, blind to their own reality. By getting to know and understand ourselves through our actions, through evaluation of our activities, we are able to compare our practice with our ideals and values. We experience a sense of reconciliation when we accept who we are and cease to struggle with self-reification. We reach a more harmonious relationship with our lived realities when we learn to accept the truth.

Talking about and articulating the practical evidence, arguing for one's interpretation, validating it, finding a rationale and a reason for the activities are essential to understand and defend one's practice. An interpretive discourse will lead to the identification of new 'self-related theories' of teaching and learning over which one has ownership.

Rogers reminds us: 'We cannot teach another person directly; we can only facilitate his learning' (Rogers 1951: 151). As the action research process proceeds, the teacher researcher and the research participants become aware of the self-referential nature of their beliefs, values and practices. 'A person learns only those things which he or she perceives as being related to himself' (Rogers 1951: 153). This is clearly a premise for forming a personal relationship with learning and the investigation of one's professional practice. Understanding develops from personal identification with the issues, the evidence and the values related to their interpretation.

Without personal involvement in learning we simply reproduce the existing hegemony through the repetition of traditional orthodoxy. Existing institutions can withstand many forms of investigation but will weaken when faced with insider action based on passionately held convictions. Understanding of self allows the researcher to explore the relationship between what she believes and what she holds as firm knowledge. This may be contradictory to the different social and educational research orthodoxies surrounding the nature of knowledge and inquiry for inclusive practice.

We can gain a new insight into the reasons why we act as we do. Learning to rely on one's own judgements rather than on other people's judgements is a necessary skill for good teacher researchers. Recognizing when one is acting out of weakness rather than out of strength is necessary to self-knowledge. Self-knowledge gives one confidence to know when and how to take calculated risks. It challenges whether risky action is taken for the benefit of the teacher researcher personally, for career advancement, for institutional kudos, or to improve inclusive practice for children and young people. Such crucial distinctions should be implicit in all research projects.

Keeping a journal

Keeping a journal is a means of deepening self-understanding and developing self-evaluation. The journal is a form of case study that provides the opportunity to explore individual personal values, beliefs and prejudices. What is important is not the fact that each individual teacher researcher brings their own experience and biography to the investigation, but more that it is recognized and acknowledged as part of the research process. Ways of controlling bias must be explored by the teacher researcher and made evident to the research participants and readers of the completed research record.

To begin with, the journal could be used to explore the reason why the research topic or focus was chosen. Is it a purely professional reason or is there a personal dimension? For example, if someone chooses to research the topic of dyslexia, it may be because they were designated as dyslexic at school. The personal relationship to the research focus brings with it emotions, feelings and insider knowledge. Often bullying and/or school failure have been personally experienced by researchers (see Lynn's case study in Chapter 4), which motivates them to investigate similar topics in adulthood. When a research focus involves strong feelings and insider experience, these must be reflexively explored within the research context. Whether or not the public account should include a reflexive rationale is debatable. Any value or attitudinal changes can be acknowledged and developed through the keeping of a journal or diary and shared with a trusted colleague or tutor. The sharing in itself can act as a form of control against non-reflexive activities and unrecognized value bias.

There is no one designated method of keeping a journal. All that is required is the ability to make a record of significant events, ideas and one's understanding of the professional issues that are part of the investigation of inclusive practice. However, because of the complex and varied nature of educational investigation, teacher researchers must be allowed the freedom to write and express their experiences in their own individual and idiosyncratic manner. A journal is primarily a vehicle for the retrospective recording of professional and personal experiences. It can be used to record facts, impressions, feelings and interpretations. It may, in time, develop into a record of interpretive and analytical notes that describes the professional's development through the research process. The journal is a means of acknowledging the writer's value position in the face of contradictory evidence. By making personal values explicit in the journal, they are therefore made visible for later reflection, either privately for the author alone or more publicly in group sharing sessions. Participating in reflective discussion with colleagues and with professional group members allows values and assumptions in the practical reality to be challenged, compared, confirmed or reconstructed. As the journal becomes more reflective, the writers become more reflexive and aware of what is actually happening to them and the inferences of their planned changes.

Practitioner action research and reflective writing are parallel activities. The journal is an unstructured, free flowing, individuated blend of concrete and interpreted reality. It is mainly unassessed in most formal higher education course contexts, but it is an essential supplement to the teacher researcher's main case study, explaining their personal educational development and active intervention for improved inclusive practice.

Everyone begins with their own personal view of a situation. How their views change and develop over time is an aspect of the research process that enriches the research account. Feelings, emotions and heart-felt passion need to be acknowledged and shared, as they may be providing the driving force for the research project. If feelings are not recognized, supported and validated they may be overlooked as an important basis for the action. How much personal reflection is eventually included in the written account, case record or thesis is a matter of its relevance to the judgements and decisions taken within the action research process.

Journal writing enables teacher researchers to find their own story and to use it as a valid basis for their own ethnographic evidence. The personal narrative is especially suitable for the construction of a professional self-identity, which is that of an individual in relationship to society, to the creation and per-petuation of professional norms and to the dynamics of power relations between professionals, colleagues, pupils and others.

In writing a journal we can identify the meaning of our experiences that constitute reality. How we perceive reality is an interpretation of the evidence presented to us – a kind of unreality – a personal reality. We act on our perceptions because this is the only way we can know and learn. Therefore, our actions depend upon:

• how we perceive ourselves;
• how we perceive the situation;
• the interrelationship between the above.

Our awareness and self-knowledge are increased through writing, because it brings to a conscious level much that is unspoken knowledge. It provides a permanent record of the research process. It helps the writer to organize the research material into themes and patterns over time. The ongoing database that the journal provides can be a resource in group meetings and discussions. It supports the author in the search for discrepancies between their role, responsibilities, power and control, and the real and the ideal in their practice. It can contribute to a person's autobiography or life history. Keeping a journal also enables the author to explore multiple realities, which only time and different perspectives make possible. The journal documents the many voices that shape practice, including the writer's and the multiple realities, selves and minds that contribute to inclusive practices.

A distinction is often made between a diary, a log and a journal. A diary may be described as an open-ended, personal and interpretive form of writing, unlike a log, which records facts related to particular concrete events. A journal is a combination of both the log and the diary, and its contents are seen as more comprehensive than those of either a log or a diary.

> It is a reconstruction of experience and, like the diary, has both objective and subjective dimensions, but unlike most diaries, there is a conscious-ness of this differentiation. In a journal, the writer can carry on a dialogue between and among various dimensions of experience.
>
> (Holly 1984)

The teacher researcher's journal, used as a support in professional develop-ment, becomes an important source of reflective evidence for professional reconstruction.

When the teacher researcher is improving inclusive school practice, the written dialogue in the journal is primarily focused on the person as an agent of change, who analyses the significant professional experiences that he or she considers relevant to that purpose. Generally, these experiences are school-centred. Occasionally, more personal experiences may emerge when writing becomes more reflexive. As the journal becomes more reflexive, the teacher researcher becomes aware of what is actually happening as a result of his or her professional intervention. This form of writing draws out the teacher's intuitive knowledge and makes them aware of what they had sensed but could not fully explain until drawn out through the conscious process of journal writing.

How to get started writing a journal

The first problem experienced is how to get started. What exactly does one write in the journal? Finding the time, developing a technique and the materials to be used become secondary to concerns about the central focus of the journal. To get started, it helps simply to write about a recent working day, or to answer the following questions:

- Was inclusion a priority in my practice today?
- What action did I take to enable better inclusive practice? Why?
- Explain further with concrete description.

Or:

- What can I record about my professional practice today?
- How did the daily events reinforce my view of myself as a teacher or professional who supports inclusive practice? Why?

By answering these deceptively simple questions, teacher researchers are in fact recalling living personal data and evaluating it. They are acting as observers of their own situation and personally reflecting on their role, recalling their own personal experience through recent concrete examples. The data are collected, practices are examined and interpreted. The journal continues to be used as a log, and as a means of exploring and reflecting on the educational issues raised. It is crucial to learn about oneself through the cataloguing of events, relevant data and personal responses, whether perceived as emotional or intellectual. The more lucid and reflexive the journal becomes, the more transparent the action research case study becomes. The more comprehensive and extensive the journal, the easier it becomes for colleagues and others to offer direction and support, and to understand the teacher's individual struggle to identify and interpret their own particular inclusive challenges. All teachers benefit from writing journals, but not everyone learns to use them effectively as written case studies in themselves.

The journal can be organized under specific headings that help to identify forms of data and to differentiate between evidence, interpretation, thoughts, ideas, reflections and feelings. For example, the following headings are often used:

Research data and evidence
Critical incidents
Pupils' responses
My responses
Ideas and reflection
My feelings
Action planned

Action taken
Results of action.

The journal would normally show a progression from a simple beginning to a more complex in-depth description, reflection and explanation of ideas, thoughts and actions as follows.

From

- asking oneself why the chosen topic or issue is relevant or worthwhile;
- recording initial feelings, attitudes and thoughts related to the research focus.

To

- finding out more about the issue;
- identifying inherent values in activities by uncovering hidden assumptions in the data;
- reflecting on one's basic beliefs about inclusive practices;
- identifying further questions from the evidence and reflection;
- recognizing one's basic personal values or feelings in the written account or journal.

To

- taking action towards greater clarification of the topic or issue through the wider and deeper search for evidence;
- honestly comparing the research evidence, ideas, beliefs and values originally held;
- identifying contradictions in values, ideas and activities related to your and others' perceptions;
- noting surprises or unexpected evidence confirming or disconfirming beliefs and expectations;
- explaining how the evidence is contributing to new perceptions;
- planning for change through appropriate means;
- anticipating the outcomes of planned action;
- monitoring interventions and collecting evidence as changes are taking place;
- reflecting on feedback from participants and colleagues by using the journal as a basis for collaboration, shared action and interpretive discourse.

Writing a journal is clarifying ideas and sharing views with a wider audience through the medium of print. It takes a certain kind of writing technology, style and skill. In order to write we need intention, purpose and word knowledge. We need something to say, we need thoughts and we need appropriate words and expressions for communicating these thoughts. This is further complicated by the fact that writing is culture-specific (Vygotsky 1978). A journal is written, and not necessarily to be spoken. The act of writing allows one the time to think, to consider and to construct the discourse before committing oneself to a kind of permanent record. Talk is transitory, and fleeting; writing is recording, it is the culmination of expression, intended for an audience. The journal is primarily for oneself, it is a form of discourse with oneself for future reflection. There is a dialogue taking place, because every written text has a hypothetical reader; and a text written for oneself when reread creates a different dialogue because of the new context and the forward movement of time (O'Hanlon 1991). Yet it is also a means of sharing professional change with others in a group engaging in interpretive discourse.

The practitioner researcher must write for and about themselves, but with another audience in mind. One cannot adjust the discourse immediately, as one does when talking, because it is fixed for subsequent readers. It has a permanence and an outward character that solidifies personal reflections in print, for oneself to consider later. It is not real conversation, yet it provides a basis for further conversation and discourse.

The uses and functions of writing vary from culture to culture and within the same society over time. It is not just the act of writing itself that is difficult for many teacher researchers; it is the transposition of their thoughts and views into print that is often the major barrier for them. It is the act of sharing the 'I' with the 'other' that forms the basis of the problem. Bakhtin (cited in Nystrand 1986) was keenly aware of this issue. He wrote that all language is inherently dialogic. Not only are the basic tools for communication social in origin, but the choices we make at every turn are shaped by the balance our language must strike between what we have to say and the context in which the text must function. This is true not only of talk, but also of ostensibly monologic forms of discourse, such as writing, including journal writing.

There may be a genuine reluctance to find the real 'I' to communicate with and about and to share with others. There is also the question of the possible leaking of confidential information to others when sharing journal writing. The discourse may be confined by lack of collegial trust and an established personal privacy boundary, which makes it very unlikely that teacher researchers will always consistently use their journal as a form of creative expression in interpretive discourse. However, the problem can be overcome if we are aware of it acting as a constraint. There are many reasons why many people are reluctant to plunge into reflective writing. Even as we write biographically, we find that we learn as much about ourselves and our circumstances as we do about others. Yet we may not want to share this self-knowledge with others.

The reluctance to start and to commit oneself to reflective writing in a professional journal is complex, but one thing is clear – you expose yourself within the situation. Becoming reflexive through writing brings about a deeper knowledge of oneself and the context in which one is acting. It is a risky business because biographical reflections allow a problem to be addressed only when it becomes visible, and if the socio-political situation allows it to emerge safely. A subtle coercion in language and expression takes place within certain formal educational contexts. Teacher researchers who share evidence from journals with colleagues or others may be raising issues related to their institutions through their own reflective journal writing. When they bring their journal to a collegial group they are developing a practical discourse about inclusive practice that becomes bound within yet another institutional context. A documentary mediation takes place subsequently and continuously through the writing of a journal, because the journal writer and the institution operate on different referential levels. They have their own language forms and functions specific to each setting. Therefore, the interpretive discourse activated by the journal is different from the original discourse recorded in writing.

The discourse is taking place on two levels, at the personal level through the journal, and at the public level through the discourse emerging from the journal writing.

A professional journal is not like a private journal, it has a professional audience in mind from its inception. A teacher researcher must share its contents, in some form, in order to activate the interpretive discourse and feedback as a reflexive debate. Yet disclosure carries risks. The question remains as to how issues related to emotional and rational control can be opened up and explored in an safe environment that supports personal disclosure. A research or focus group can provide such a context if it operates through sensitive, confidential, democratic and inclusive procedures. The journal can emerge as a case study, when teacher researchers become more confident with its purposes and value, and understand its potential for self and professional development. Teacher researchers who excel in terms of self-development and reflexive thinking, and who change their institutions, making them more inclusive, often share their journal with others in a consistently open and authentic manner. They become less concerned about a wider audience and learn to trust their colleagues to interpret their professional concerns.

Anna

Anna, the teacher in the story that follows, has been writing a reflective journal, which uncovers self-knowledge, leading to a re-evaluation of her professional practice. She is surprised by her research findings and changes her attitudes to, and views about, mainstream schooling. Anna felt initially that pupils with special educational needs could not be satisfactorily or fully educated in mainstream schools. These are her journal extracts.

Defining my research question was not an easy process. I have worked in the special education sector for most of my career as a teacher and I have clearly developed a good understanding of pupils with special educational needs. I perhaps have become a little too self-assured of my own abilities to teach pupils with SEN over time and have developed a bias in favour of special schools and, by default, against mainstream schooling for these pupils.

I am conscious, however, that local changes in special schooling are pending. I know that changes are planned to broaden the inclusive practice of the school. Pupils from mainstream schools are being included in our school and our pupils are also attending sessional placements in mainstream schools. Colleagues from mainstream schools are visiting the school regularly, seeking advice on named pupils with SEN. Looking at the existing school practice I feel that we are adequately meeting the needs of our pupils and any changes would be disruptive. But when I meet mainstream colleagues and talk to them, I gain a greater understanding of the LEA's intentions for developing inclusive practice for pupils with SEN. Through my investigation I am seeing the school in a more objective way. We seem to be doing 'inclusive work' for pupils outside the school, but what is happening for our own pupils? Are they experiencing an inclusive education?

On reflection, my research question is: 'How far do the existing systems and procedures in the school inhibit or encourage the development of inclusive opportunities for its pupils?'

I have been a teacher for more than ten years and have had experience of teaching in mainstream. Yet what is very clear to me is how pro-special schooling I am. My own prejudice is clear. I have grave doubts about mainstream schools being able to successfully teach children with SEN.

The action research is progressing and I feel more sympathetic to the enormous constraints that mainstream teachers are under through the National Curriculum, particularly in the secondary sector. I am also beginning to understand that the needs of many pupils in the SEN sector are not necessarily going to be met through special schooling.

I have arrived at a crossroads in my understanding and ask myself, how can the educational needs of pupils with SEN be best met? Where can they be best met and by whom? What prevents and what facilitates this happening? School changes are already being planned, and some sessional placements have begun in the mainstream school for our pupils. Several threads are weaving together as a focus for my action research. What is the school staff's understanding of the changes planned? What systems and procedures in school would enable these changes to take place or perhaps constrain them?

I want to find out what the attitudes of the staff are to the proposed change, and what ideas they have about its facilitation. I feel the best way to collect the initial data is via a questionnaire because of time constraints. I will talk to everyone on the staff and explain the purpose of the research. I will also interview the inclusion coordinator to find if there is a disparity between the staff's view of inclusion initiatives and the school's aims and objectives.

I will observe one pupil's sessional placement in a mainstream school because a pupil in my own class has just begun some mainstream inclusion in a school nearby.

Interpretation of the questionnaires shows that staff think that some, but not all, pupils would benefit greatly from mainstream placement, but it is essential to provide adequate support.

Advantages listed by staff are as follows:

- raised self-esteem;
- access to different resources;
- academic stimulation in specific curriculum areas;
- positive relationships with mainstream peers in their locality;
- broadening pupils' overall experience.

Disadvantages listed by staff are:

- possible lowered self-esteem;
- staffing difficulties;
- timetabling repercussions;
- loss of curriculum entitlement;
- time lost in travel;
- potential language and communication difficulties;
- financial implications;
- confusion and unfamiliarity for pupils;
- possible bullying;
- pupils' increased sense of feeling different.

Teachers are concerned that they would be supporting mainstream colleagues, accommodating more mainstream pupils in the special school on a sessional basis and teaching a more permanent core of pupils with complex and severe learning difficulties. However, there are some very constructive suggestions about how to facilitate inclusive practice in the school, as follows:

- to arrange preliminary visits for staff to mainstream schools;
- to support pupils in preparing for visits and also in debriefing after their inclusive mainstream sessions;
- to create greater informal links between schools, e.g. sporting events;
- to arrange regular meetings between schools;
- to provide continuity of teaching approaches for both staff and pupils;
- to have clear and shared educational objectives for placements;
- to arrange reciprocal visits for staff and pupils from special and mainstream schools;
- to provide adequate time for all staff involved to ensure effective time management;
- to provide appropriate support and effective communication between schools;
- to ensure close and regular monitoring of placements;
- to provide adequate cover for staff, especially classroom assistants supporting pupils on inclusion placements;
- to provide joint staff training days between mainstream and special schools;
- to provide a school INSET day for all staff to clarify the future of inclusive practice between mainstream and special schools.

These recommendations are invaluable to the staff and detailed planning of the aims and records of experimental sessions will be monitored for regular review and revision. Additional evidence of positive attitudes towards inclusive practice are provided by the school's inclusion coordinator. She says, 'Ultimately, I would like to see every child having an opportunity to spend time in mainstream school. As soon as children start our school, it will be built in and will become the norm rather than something we think about later as an *add on*.'

She explains how there are issues around sessional placement for pupils with complex needs or older pupils. There are concerns about missed sessions in the 'home' school. She feels that starting up a new initiative such as this is fraught with problems because it isn't built into the existing school system. She is disappointed at the school staff's response to her repeated requests to identify pupils who would benefit from mainstream opportunities. She identified potential constraints to her initiatives as follows:

• mainstream staff focus on their own curriculum areas and not seeing the whole curriculum in a more creative way;
• timetabling and missed sessions in the 'home' school are a problem;
• staff confidence is lacking because few staff have experience of mainstream practice;
• transport has to deal with greater distances between schools and the time involved in moving from one school to another, given the wide catchment area of the 'home' school;
• schools have management and organizational constraints.

She feels that 'schools have to be receptive and not all schools are receptive to children being included. The sessional placements have to be successful, we can't have kids failing. They've already failed once in the mainstream, they can't fail again.'

She wants more discussion with the staff to convince them of the potential behind inclusion, rather than seeing only the problems. She wants the special school staff to gain a mainstream perspective to appreciate the different pressures facing mainstream colleagues. 'It means people getting together and learning from each other!' She is very interested in the responses to the questionnaire and is basing much of her future planning on it. She is planning a major initiative for more inclusive practice next term. She is planning to talk to staff and pupils in advance of placements to help to counteract any anxieties they are experiencing. It is planned that pupils will in future make visits to schools before placements. They will initially be supported, but then support from teachers and classroom assistants will be withdrawn once it appears to be working. Parents and pupils will also be involved in discussions to determine the most appropriate educational provision. 'I would hope that pupils themselves are going to flag up that they would like some time in mainstream schools, now that they know they have the opportunity to do so.'

Hannah, who has Down's syndrome, is presently attending sessions in a local mainstream school. Some of the issues related to the support of Hannah's mainstream placement recorded are:

13 October

> It is the logistics of inclusion that are going to prove so difficult. One of my pupils is due to start inclusion work at her local primary school after half term, because it is written in her 'Statement of SEN', and her parents are the driving force behind the move. She will be doing an art lesson, missing history and personal and social education at her special school due to the travelling. She will repeat art on Fridays here with me. She needs to be supported in her sessions by a classroom assistant (CA). The two CAs who work with me and the class are the obvious choice to accompany her. However, one doesn't drive and the other hasn't got a car, but does drive. She also has a second job, which means she must leave promptly at 3.15 p.m. Hannah will have to be supported by another CA who doesn't know her. This will have a knock-on effect of disrupting the class here, because the CA will be taken from it. She will be replaced by a supply CA,

but what a lot of organizational upheaval for one pupil doing one mainstream inclusion session!

21 November

Hannah starts her inclusion work tomorrow. A CA from Year 6 has agreed to escort her there. One of my CAs will accompany them this week, but will leave in time to get to her second job. She will drive the school minibus. A supply CA will cover in school, but is yet to be appointed. Hannah's mum has been contacted and is pleased with the arrangements. Hannah's target will be to converse with pupils in mainstream school and rekindle friendships with her peers in mainstream, many of whom she already knows.

23 November

Hannah's first session went well. She was a little apprehensive on arrival, and again when her familiar CA left. However, she soon settled in with her new CA and recognized a boy she knew in the classroom. The other children enjoyed having her there and treated her well.

29 November

Another successful session is over! We've done lots of reinforcement this week to prepare Hannah for her inclusion sessions. She associates going to mainstream with the fact that her Mummy meets her at the school. She was less nervous this time and coped well with the art activity set for the class. Next week her CA won't go. It will be the replacement CA and we will prepare Hannah for that.

7 December

Hannah coped well without her familiar CA. She was a little quiet to begin with but accepted her new CA's guidance, although after a while she told her to go away because she could do it by herself.

Hannah feels that her CA is an unnecessary impediment in a mainstream situation and wants to remain in the art lesson unsupported, like the other mainstream pupils. Reading her story and reflecting on her experience, I find parallels between my own responses and values and those of the staff. I find this very enlightening and am working towards reversing the preconceptions I held prior to embarking on the action research.

Staff are generally in favour of pupils being given opportunities in mainstream. They are, however, concerned that a support structure or system should be put in place to ensure productive and quality mainstream experiences for our pupils. If a structure is not put in place and the placements are not prepared and organized well, with appropriate resourcing, then there will be a definite sense that the experiences are superficial at best for everyone concerned. However, the special school staff also want more information about what is going to happen, because they feel that these initiatives are forced from above. In fact, one teacher puts the reservations felt by everyone succinctly when she says, 'Vitally, we need to open a discussion of what is happening and what is intended to happen. This actually, in my experience, has not been done. It is a scheme being applied almost covertly. Only with more openness will issues be worked on efficiently.'

Another teacher asks that staff be 'put in the picture as to what their role will be and to ensure that everyone understands what is happening to avoid wholesale panic – to be totally open'.

When I compare the school's aims and objectives with the evidence from the questionnaires there isn't such a disparity between the two as I originally foresaw. What is evident is that neither staff as individuals nor the school as an institution want the pupils to experience failure in mainstream. What both sides have in common is that any and all inclusion initiatives need to be carefully considered, and organized according to pupils' needs. Both sides want more discussion about plans before proceeding and they want more training for better understanding of the issues involved.

A deliberate action that I propose is that the inclusion coordinator and the staff meet regularly for discussions about what is planned through the LEA. The time is right to engage staff with a more active participation in this vision for the future. Staff in the school do not fully understand where their own practice is leading because they are not fully aware of the policy driving it. The meetings and discussions are arranged for the new year to concentrate on improving the staff's understanding of the inclusion initiative. A school in-service day will be arranged, detailing the LEA's review of provision for pupils with SEN. The LEA will have the opportunity to share its aims and objectives and to explain the increased role for staff in aiding greater mainstream opportunities for special school pupils. Staff are also sharing details of current placements and providing information about pupils on inclusive placements between schools, which is to become a regular feature on the agenda of whole staff and departmental meetings.

The journal record above was written by a teacher researcher who works in a special school. While detailed, it omits much primary evidence and the actual feedback from colleagues through extended discussions and debate.

Anna began with a preconceived view about inclusion, but she changed her perceptions through the action research process. In doing research, in deliberating about information and evidence, she witnesses personal changes, because she is in fact changing herself. The demonstration of that change lies in her school initiatives and plans for action. The actions demonstrate in some way a change in the position of the teacher researcher, as well as a different view of the researched 'situation'. She concludes with evaluation of the action taken, which she is continuing with the support of the headteacher and colleagues in the school. School-wide change for improved inclusive practice has been brought about through both personal and professional change.

CHAPTER NINE

Moving towards more inclusive educational practice

Research is more than intelligent action or reflective practice
. . . it requires a context of openness, public scrutiny and
criticism.

(Pring 2000: 138)

The emphasis of this book has been on interpretive discourse through a democratic and inclusive methodology for the advancement of inclusive practice.
However, in learning the basic research skills, you may require some support
or training before you can use them. This could be undertaken through short
LEA in-service training sessions, or through longer-term postgraduate courses
in higher education. It could also be achieved through a kind of learning on
the job, in contexts where action research is valued and the expertise exists to
support teachers and other professionals to learn the techniques. An informal
permanent action research culture is propagated in some educational institutions, where the commitment of senior staff to action research is a way of life.
It becomes a form of curriculum development through whole-school evaluation. It may take time to achieve results, but it creates an organic evolving
school with aims and ideals shared and owned by staff, parents and pupils.

Every educational professional or teacher is responsible for influencing
inclusive practice. They all, through their professional roles, talk and act in
ways that demonstrate their attitudes to inclusive practice. They can make it
better and they can make it happen in a multitude of subtle ways in their
everyday lives. Even if they don't succeed in what they intend to achieve, they
are still influencing the situation in ways they cannot estimate or predict. This
should not stop them trying to change the negative attitudes of others and
to do their best to empower marginalized pupils through education. Inclusive
practice should evaluate the current experiences of pupils on the margins. We
should ensure that the educational experiences of all pupils are of high quality,
regardless of whether they are located in special or mainstream schools. We
need to ask parents and pupils about how they view schooling and whether it

meets their definitions and standards for inclusive practice. We need to investigate when education in a special school is viewed as successful but may or may not use inclusive strategies. Alternatively, education in a mainstream school may be viewed as successful, but may need to develop more inclusive strategies. A successful education and an inclusive education may require different educational strategies to achieve their aims, but inclusive practices need to be good educational practices. The criteria often used to evaluate inclusive practice rest upon socializing factors that exclude academic considerations because they are impossible to assess comparatively in relation to different school contexts.

I have deliberately avoided being dogmatic in relation to what exactly needs to be addressed in different educational contexts. This can only be decided by people on the ground working with children, young people and adults on the margins of society who are not fully accessing its goods. The priorities of a class teacher, a headteacher, an LEA officer, social worker or educational psychologist will differ in relation to individual professional precedent, but their overarching aims for inclusion can be shared. The locations and themes in Table 3.1 give some indicators for a possible action research focus.

Action research for inclusive practice can be carried out in a variety of ways:

- individually and informally in educational situations;
- individually within a formal support structure, e.g. by attending an LEA course or university programme;
- collaboratively through informal groupings of colleagues in an institutional context;
- collaboratively through a formal arrangement with like-minded professionals, like a research group in the LEA or university;
- informally in an institution like a school, where whole-school evaluation is prioritizing inclusive practice;
- formally in any institution, e.g. a school that resources continuing professional development for individual teachers.

Professional change is the basis of any systemic or structural change related to inclusive practice in schools and educational contexts. Institutional change can begin through the action and commitment of a single individual (see Meg's case study in Chapter 3), through an increase in one's self-awareness and self-evaluation despite the experience of initial failure (see Shona's case study in Chapter 4), or by changing one's attitude to inclusion (see Anna's case study in Chapter 8). We must be wary of using practices that we believe are 'inclusive' simply because others suggest they are.

The focus on professional autonomy and reflective practice might suggest a liberal approach to practice, but discursive and interpretive feedback between the research participants, before plans are implemented, defends against hasty misjudgements. When practitioner researchers are involved in making judgements about what change is worthwhile and significant, and when new practices and ways of thinking are introduced into the dialogue, then standards of professional effectiveness are questioned and problematized – and ultimately negotiated before they are influenced and changed.

To think about practice as activity embedded within theory is important in thinking about changing teaching and professional inclusive practice. The degree to which teacher researchers engage in a dialogue concerning good practice and justify taking control of their classroom and school activities is critical to good inclusive practice. So, too, is evaluating how these justifications relate to the socially constructed standards of good inclusive practice. Making justifications involves reflection on professional inclusive activities and their theoretical frameworks, and an ability to articulate them in a meaningful way. Research, then, should provide practitioners not just with findings in the form of activities or behaviours that work, but also with ways of thinking and empirical evidence related to teaching and learning for inclusion. Opportunities should be created to allow professionals to interact and have conversations about what they consider to be good inclusive practice. Necessary in the conversations are discussions of alternative ideas and activities that, in combination with some of the professional's own perceptions, form a view of good inclusive practice.

Everyday working principles that underlie inclusive activities can be made explicit and subject to critique through interpretive discourse. Theories of how we operate in the way we do, the constraints on our ideals and the gap between rhetoric and reality need to be expressed and debated both locally and nationally. However, these practical, inclusive ideas and theories are embedded in more general inclusive theories in our culture. This makes them difficult to extricate, because they are embedded in a historical text that demands collective deconstruction before we can fully understand them. The deconstruction may not necessarily lead to the development of universal principles for inclusive practice. The search for understanding is motivated by a practical problem, like how to prevent one pupil's exclusion, about which decisions must be made. Educational traditions are living changing traditions related to current forms of inclusive practices that are still evolving. They speak differently to each person in the present moment and are dependent on the individual person's experience, background and understanding.

Teacher and practitioner researchers bring their own theories to bear on the understanding of the situation, because there are no general structures of rationality to appeal to that constitute understanding. This does not mean that there are no criteria for making judgements about the quality of inclusive practices. The criteria are created in negotiation with other participants in the situational context, with particular relevance to the research focus or question. However, a critique for understanding will always be limited by a person's standpoint, openness and responsiveness to the issue under investigation. It is in the research communication, conversation and discourse that interpretations are developed and confirmed through the sharing of evidence, perceptions and ideas. There is an inextricable connection between understanding and communication. Interpretive reflection can only emerge through dialogue. It needs communities of discursive practitioners to engage in dialogue on the crucial issues of inclusive practice. These discursive interpretive and democratic communities, to be inclusive, must include the voices of all those concerned, especially the most vulnerable, children and young people.

People occupy different positions within discursive practices, positions that are produced by the power and knowledge relations of particular discourses like inclusion. The teacher researcher exists in the research process as a partial voice occupying a site or position that may itself be contradictory. Issues related to inclusive practice need to be problematized rather than 'solved' to see how the situation or problem was structured in the first place.

The aims and quality of inclusive educational practice must be constantly monitored and reviewed through the open exposure of problems and constraints. Education is not immutable and unchanging. It cannot be a palliative for all of society's problems. Yet in educational contexts social problems when raised and debated become a democratic means of recognizing and sharing moral concerns related to concepts like 'equality' or 'inclusion'. The aims of education are critical to the understanding of educational equality and equal opportunity. In the determination of educational quality no conception of equality will be adequately grounded unless the aims are well grounded. In aiming to distribute resources fairly we cannot at the same time distribute universally.

Inclusive practice must always be good educational practice. It has been noted that a bad education contributes to the risk or the likelihood of criminality, to the extent that someone is socially marginalized within and beyond the school. It includes the quality of teacher–student relationships, which is also recognized to be related to the crime rate in schools (Curren 1995). A bad education can also influence a young person's employment and socio-economic status, and unemployment is a significant predictor for criminality, as is low status in a highly stratified society.

Alternatively, equity is believed to be a matter of human and physical resources, and inclusion may be transformed into an enterprise of risk management, where the severity of the pupil's impairment is offset against a resource allocation to maintain the institutional equilibrium of the school (Slee 1996). Resources ought to be used to support schools' development as enabling cultures mediated through their curriculum organization, teaching methodologies and extracurricular activities. The use of resources to boost the assimilation of diverse pupil groups in mainstream schools needs to be challenged. The mere assimilation of pupils *per se* may be a guise for inclusion and hides the issues of unequal power relations in the politics of institutional practice.

Pupil diversity and difference in any educational context strengthen and widen the educational culture. An increase in access to teacher and professional training for the creation of greater human professional diversity needs to take place in parallel with increasing pupil inclusion, in order to provide role models for diverse and different pupils.

The term difference or different is fluid, and captures the problems inherent in any categorization of pupils in educational contexts. Difference is a profound feature of self-experience. It can be a contradictory concept and one that, educationally, can lead to misunderstanding. Certain differences are not neutral, but are permeated with power differentials that divide us beyond the limit of language and our ability to understand them (Lyotard 1988). These factors lead us to feel a tension with other educational values and aims. While we can learn from these tensions, the disruption that difference brings has provoked educators to resolve the tension by a quick fix or by clinging to guidelines, programmes or curricula that assure some stability in the situation. All difference in education is viewed from the perspective of a given framework of understanding, such as SEN, often without regard for the very different meaning felt by this differentiation from the perspective of the person or group referred to. When differences are defined and decisions are based on their significance, they are potentially harmful. A critique of difference in schools has enabled educators, parents and pupils alike to question what significant differences mean in certain situations, whether they are visible or whether they really matter. It has led to a questioning of where such structures of reference come from, and how they gain their power. It has led to people realizing that small or trivial differences may be related to larger, more significant differences, so that working on small, apparently trivial differences through action research may influence and improve large and significant differences. It has led people to realize that all difference is constructed and not inherent, so that it can always be reconstructed in another way. Social and educational differences are magnified or decreased by practice in various situations. We all, by implication, share responsibility for changing and specifying their meanings through educational practice. Education is not simply about transmitting an existing system of values and beliefs, unchanged, from one generation to the next. There must be room for questioning, discussing, reinterpreting and modifying educational differences, and understanding where they fit in the context of a richly diverse, rapidly changing world. There is a need for an interpretive, discursive, inclusive and democratic investigatory process to keep abreast of necessary social change.

The situations to be transformed are often of a complex nature, requiring the reconstruction of educational institutions, so it is necessary to possess reliable knowledge about how such institutions work. Every inquirer is also able to formulate assertions about how to reconstruct such situations. It requires a fallible rather than a dogmatic disposition, which follows the evidence of the inquiry wherever it leads, rather than clinging to preconceived ideas. Experimental inquiry is the basis of a democratic life, which implies both a willingness to entertain novel ideas and the personal flexibility to carry out new ways of perceiving and acting.

The power to move professionals and others away from exclusionary practice resides in affording them the possibility of a pedagogy that uncovers and reduces inequality. For many this will mean exposing and examining institutional structures that exert an oppressive force. For others it may lead to making explicit certain rules within institutions that provide pupils with opportunities for fuller participation. Pedagogical approaches derived from action research foster an understanding of position in relation to others and to social institutions, in which the root causes of inequality are exposed and examined. It is important that educational practices provide opportunities for understanding that knowledge is partial, socially and culturally constructed. We need opportunities to develop new awareness through a deeper interpretation of the discourses of power, privilege and agency, to create ameliorating pedagogical practices for inclusion.

Finally, this book urges professionals and teachers who use action research for more inclusionary practice to approach teaching, teacher education and professional practice in a similar manner. It prompts all educators to develop reflective practice in their work with those who share similar values and thus become lifelong discursive educators. It encourages practitioner researchers to use action research as an ameliorating philosophy, where responsibilities for fair and equitable practice are seen as socially constructed in the interactive process of education and social practice. The whole school and its wider community must be involved in the process of change for a better school system, which counteracts injustice and alienation within its institutions. The amelioration of contradictory practices and actions is inherently an aspect of ongoing, lifelong learning. The individual and community learning gained from teacher research processes need wider dissemination, public awareness and understanding to impact powerfully on all educational contexts, and to influence the wider society.

References

Adelman, C. (1993) Kurt Lewin and the origins of action research, *Education Action Research Journal*, 1(1): 7–25.

Ainscow, M. (1999) *Understanding the Development of Inclusive Schools*. London: Falmer Press.

Ainscow, M., Booth, T. and Dyson, A. (1999) Inclusion and exclusion: listening to some hidden voices, in K. Ballard (ed.) *Inclusion and Exclusion in Education and Society: Voices on Disability and Justice*. London: Falmer Press.

Altrichter, H., Posch, P. and Somekh, B. (1993) *Teachers Investigate Their Work*. London: Routledge.

Aristotle (1955) *Ethics* (trans. J.A.K. Thomson). London: Penguin Classics.

Bakhtin, M. (1981) *The Dialogic Imagination: Four Essays*. Austin: University of Texas Press.

Baldwin, M. (2000) *Care Management and Community Care: Social Work Discretion and the Construction of Policy*. Aldershot: Ashgate.

Barton, L. (ed.) (1987) *The Politics of Special Educational Needs*. Lewes: Falmer Press.

BERA (1992) *Ethical Guidelines in Research*. Edinburgh: British Educational Research Association.

Bernstein, B. (1971) *Class, Codes and Control: Theoretical Studies toward Sociology of Language*. London: Routledge and Kegan Paul.

Biggs, J. and Telfer, R. (1987) *The Process of Learning*, 2nd edn. Sydney: Prentice Hall.

Bogdan, R. and Biklin, S. (1982) *Qualitative Research in Education*. Boston: Allyn and Bacon.

Booth, T. and Ainscow, M. (eds) (1998) *From them to us: an international study of inclusion in education*. London: Routledge.

Brock-Utne, B. (1980) What is educational action research? *Classroom Action Research Network Bulletin*, 4: 10–15.

Brown, A. and Dowling, P. (1998) *Doing Research: Reading Research*. London: Falmer Press.

BSA (1997) *The International Numeracy Survey*. London: Basic Skills Agency Resource Centre.

Burgess, R. (ed.) (1989) *The Ethics of Educational Research*. London: Falmer Press.

Calderhead, J. (1988) The development of knowledge structures in learning to teach, in J. Calderhead (ed.) *Teachers' Professional Learning*. Lewes: Falmer Press.

Carr, W. (ed.) (1987) *Quality in Teaching*. Lewes: Falmer Press.

Carr, W. and Kemmis, S. (1986) *Becoming Critical: Education, Knowledge and Action Research*. London: Falmer Press.

Clandinin, J. (1986) *Classroom Practice: Teacher Images in Action*. Lewes: Falmer Press.

Clandinin, J. and Connelly, M. (1986) Rhythms in teaching: the narrative study of teachers' personal practical knowledge of classrooms, *Teaching and Teacher Education*, 2: 377–87.

Cohen, L. and Manion, L. (1989) *Research Methods in Education*, 3rd edn. London: Routledge.

Coulthard, M. (1985) *An Introduction to Discourse Analysis*. London: Longman.

Cowne, E. (1998) *The Senco Handbook: Working within a Whole-school Approach*. London: David Fulton.

CSIE (1989) *The Integration Charter*. Bristol: Centre for Studies in Inclusive Education.

CSIE (2000) *The Inclusion Index*. Bristol: Centre for Studies in Inclusive Education.

Curren, R. (1995) Justice and the threshold of educational opportunity, in M. Katz (ed.) *Philosophy of Education*. Urbana, IL: Philosophy of Education Society.

Dadds, M. (1995) *Passionate Enquiry and School Development*. London: Falmer Press.

Day, C. (1984) Teachers thinking, intentions and practice: an action research perspective, in R. Hawkes and J. Olsen (eds) *Teacher Thinking*. Lisse: Swets and Zeitlinger.

Denzin, N.K. (1978) *The Research Act: A Theoretical Introduction to Sociological Methods*, 2nd edn. New York: McGraw-Hill.

Derrida, J. (1978) *Writing and Difference*. London: Routledge and Kegan Paul.

DES (1978) *Special Educational Needs: Report of the Committee of Enquiry into the Education of Handicapped Children and Young People* (The Warnock Report). London: HMSO.

Dewey, J. (1933) *How We Think: A Restatement of the Relation of Thinking to the Educative Process*. Lexington, MA: D.C. Heath.

Dewey, J. (1966) *Democracy and Education*. New York: The Free Press.

Dewey, J. (1974) *John Dewey on Education: Selected Writings* (ed. R.D. Archambault). Chicago: University of Chicago Press.

Dewey, J. (1990) *The School and Society: The Child and the Curriculum*. Chicago: University of Chicago Press.

DfE (1994) *Pupils' Behaviour and Discipline*. London: HMSO.

DfEE (1997a) *Permanent Exclusions from Schools*. London: Department for Education and Employment.

DfEE (1997b) *Excellence for All Children: Meeting Special Educational Needs*. London: Department for Education and Employment.

DfEE (1998a) *Meeting Special Educational Needs*. London: Department for Education and Employment.

DfEE (1998b) *Programme of Action*. London: HMSO.

DfEE (1999) *Social Inclusion: Pupil Support*, Circular 10/99. London: DfEE.

DfEE (2000a) *The Revised Code of Practice on the Identification and Assessment of Special Educational Needs*. London: HMSO.

DfEE (2000b) *The Revised National Curriculum for 2000: What Has Changed* (QCA/99/513). London: QCA.

DfES (2001) *SEN and Disability Act*. London: HMSO.

DfES (2002) *Class Sizes in Maintained Schools in England, January 2001* (www.dfee.gov.uk).

Diamond, S.C. (1995) Special education and the great god inclusion, in D.M. Kauffman and D.P. Hallahan (eds) *The Illusion of Full Inclusion: A Comprehensive Critique of a Current Special Education Bandwagon*. Austin, TX: PRO-ED.

DRC (2002) *Code of Practice for Schools: Disability Discrimination Act 1995: Part 4*. London: HMSO.

Duke, D.L. (1995) *Teacher Evaluation Policy: From Accountability to Professional Development*. Albany: State University of New York Press.

Dyson, A. (1999) Inclusion and inclusions: theories and discourses in inclusive education, in H. Daniels and P. Garner (eds) *Inclusive Education: Supporting Inclusion in Education Systems*. London: Kogan Page.

Eisner, E. (1976) Educational connoisseurship and criticism: their form and function in educational evaluation, *Journal of Aesthetic Education*, 10: 135–50.

Eisner, E. (1985) *The Educational Imagination: On Design and Evaluation of School Programs*, 2nd edn. New York: Macmillan.

Elbaz, F. (1983) *Teacher Thinking: A Study of Practical Knowledge*. New York: Nichols.

Elbaz, F. (1991) Hope, attentiveness and caring for difference: the moral voice in teaching, Paper presented at the International Study Association on Teacher Thinking, Surrey.

Elliott, J. (1981) Action research: a framework for self-evaluation in schools. Working paper no. 1, in *Teacher–Pupil Interaction and the Quality of Learning*. London: Schools Council.

Elliott, J. (1985) Educational action research, in J. Nisbet and S. Nisbet (eds) *Research Policy and Practice: World Yearbook of Education*. London: Kogan Page.

Elliott, J. (1989) Educational theory and the professional learning of teachers: an overview, *Cambridge Journal of Education*, 19: 81–101.

Elliott, J. (1991) *Action Research for Educational Change*. Buckingham: Open University Press.

Elliott, J. (1994) Research on teachers' knowledge and action research, *Education Action Research*, 2(1): 43–69.

Elliott, J. (1995a) What is good action research? Some criteria, *Action Researcher*, 2: 10–11.

Elliott, J. (1995b) Action research and the professional development of teachers: a cross European perspective, Paper presented at the Nineteenth Conference of the Association for Teacher Education in Europe, Prague, September.

Elliott, J. (1998) *The Curriculum Experiment: Meeting the Challenge of Social Change*. Buckingham: Open University Press.

Elliott, J. (2000a) Revising the National Curriculum: a comment on the Secretary of State's proposals, *Journal of Educational Policy*, 25(2): 245–55.

Elliott, J. (2000b) Doing action research: doing practical philosophy, *Prospero*, 6(3/4): 82–100.

Elliott, J. and Adelman, C. (1973) Reflecting where the action is: the design of the Ford teaching project, *Education for Teaching*, 92: 8–20.

Elliott, J. and Ebbutt, D. (1985) *Issues in Teaching for Understanding*. London: School Council/Longman.

Entwhistle, N. (1992) *The Impact of Teaching on Learning Outcomes in Higher Education*. Sheffield: CVCP Staff Development Unit.

Feldman, M. (1995) *Strategies for Interpreting Qualitative Data*. London: Sage.

Fenstermacher, G. (1986) Philosophy of research on teaching: three aspects, in M. Wittrock (ed.) *Handbook of Research on Teaching*. New York: Macmillan.

Feyerabend, P. (1975) *Against Method: Outline of an Anarchistic Theory of Knowledge*. London: Verso.

Foster, P., Gomm, R. and Hammersley, M. (1996) *Constructing Educational Inequality*. London: Falmer Press.

Friere, P. (1990) *Pedagogy of the Oppressed*. New York: Continuum.

Gadamer, H.G. (1981) *Reason in the Age of Science*. Cambridge, MA: MIT Press.

Geertz, C. (1973) Thick description: toward an interpretive theory of culture, in C. Geertz, *The Interpretation of Cultures: Selected Essays*. New York: Basic Books.

Giangreco, M., Cloninger, C., Dennis, R. and Edelman, S. (1994) Problem solving methods to facilitate inclusion education, in J. Thousand, R. Villa and A. Nevin (eds) *Creativity and Collaborative Learning: A Practical Guide to Empowering Students and Teachers*. Baltimore: Brookes.

Giddens, A. (2000) *The Third Way and Its Critics*. Cambridge: Polity Press.

Gillborn, D. and Gipps, C. (1996) *A Review of Recent Research on Achievement by Minority Ethnic Pupils*. London: Office for Standards in Education/Institute of Education.

Goodson, I. (1992) *Studying Teachers' Lives*. London: Routledge.

Goodson, I. (2001) The story of life history: origins of the life history method in sociology, *Identity: An International Journal of Theory and Research*, 1(2): 129–42.

Green, K. (1999) Defining the field of literature in action research: a personal approach, *Education Action Research Journal*, 7(1): 105–25.

Grundy, S. and Kemmis, S. (1988) Educational action research in Australia: the state of the art, in S. Kemmis and R. McTaggart (eds) *The Action Research Reader*, 3rd edn. Geelong: Deakin University Press.

Habermas, J. (1986) *The Theory of Communicative Action. Volume 1: Reason and the Rationalisation of Society*. Cambridge: Polity Press.

Harré, R. (1978) Accounts, actions and meanings – the practice of participatory psychology, in M. Brenner, P. Marsh and M. Brenner (eds) *The Social Context of Method*. London: Croom Helm.

HESA (2001) *Higher Education Statistics for the UK 1999/2000*. Cheltenham: HESA.

Hollingsworth, S. (1997) *International Action Research: A Case Book for Educational Reform*. London: Falmer Press.

Holly, M.L. (1984) *Keeping a Personal–Professional Journal*. Geelong: Deakin University Press.

Holt, J. (1982) *How Children Fail*. London: Penguin Books.

Hoyle, E. (1974) Professionality, professionalism and control in teaching, *London Educational Review*, 3: 13–19.

Hustler, D. (ed.) (1986) *Action Research in Classrooms and Schools*. London: Allen and Unwin.

James, M. and Worrall, N. (2000) Building a reflective community: development through collaboration between a higher education institution and one school over ten years, *Education Action Research Journal*, 8(1): 93–115.

Jung, C.G. (1998) *The Essential Jung*. London: Fontana.

Kemmis, S. and McTaggart, R. (eds) (1981) *The Action Research Reader*. Geelong: Deakin University Press.

Kincheloe, J.L. (1991) *Teachers as Researchers: Qualitative Inquiry as a Path to Empowerment*. London: Falmer Press.

Kuhl, J. (1982) Action vs state orientation as a mediator between motivation and action, in W. Hacker, W. Volpert and M. von Cranach (eds) *Cognitive and Motivational Aspects of Action*. Amsterdam: North-Holland.

Lewin, K. (1946) Action research and minority problems, *Journal of Social Issues*, 2: 34–46.

Lyotard, J.-F. (1988) *The Differend: Phrases in Dispute* (trans. G. van den Abbeele). Minneapolis: University of Minnesota Press.

McCutcheon, J. (2001) *Essex Inclusive Schools Project 1999–2000*. SENCO Update no. 21. London: Optimus Publishing.

MacIntyre, A. (1982) *After Virtue: A Study of Moral Theory*. London: Duckworth.

MacIntyre, A. and Dunne, J. (2002) Alisdair MacIntyre on education: in dialogue with Joseph Dunne, *Journal of Philosophy of Education*, 36(1): 1–21.

McNiff, J. (1988) *Action Research: Principles and Practice*. London: Macmillan.

McTaggart, R. and Singh, M. (1987) A fourth generation of action research: notes on the Deakin seminar, Paper presented at American Educational Research Association Conference, New Orleans.

Maslow, A. (1987) *Motivation and Personality*, 3rd edn. New York: Harper and Row.

Mill, J.S. (1929) *On Liberty*. London: Watts and Co.

Munro, P. (1998) *Subject to Fiction: Women Teachers' Life History Narratives and the Cultural Politics of Resistance*. Buckingham: Open University Press.

NASC (2001) *Norwich Area Schools Consortium Publications*. Norwich: CARE, UEA.

Nias, J. (1980) *Changing Times, Changing Identities: Grieving for a Lost Self*. Cambridge: Institute of Education.

Nixon, J. (1987) The teacher as researcher: contradictions and continuities, *Peabody Journal of Education*, 62(2): 20–32.

Nystrand, M. (ed.) (1986) *The Structure of Written Communication*. New York: Academic Press.

O'Donoghue, T. and Chalmers, R. (2000) How teachers manage their work in inclusive classrooms, *Teaching and Teacher Education*, 16(8): 889–905.

O'Hanlon, C. (1988) Facilitation and the homing pigeon: the tutor's role in educational innovation, *British Journal of In-service Education*, 14(3): 170–6.

O'Hanlon, C. (1991) A risky business? The use of diaries in teachers' action research, in C. Ryan and B. Somekh (eds) *Processes of Reflection and Action*. Norwich: CARN Publications, Centre for Applied Research in Education, University of East Anglia.

O'Hanlon, C. (1992) Testing out developmental linguistics, *English in Education*, 26(1): 48–58.

O'Hanlon, C. (1993) The Importance of an Articulated Personal Theory of Professional Development, in J. Elliott (ed.) *Reconstructing Teacher Education*, London: Falmer Press pp 243–257.

O'Hanlon, C. (1995a) (ed) *Inclusive Education in Europe*. London: David Fulton

O'Hanlon, C. (1995b) Why is action research a valid basis for professional development? in R. McBride (ed.) *Teacher Education Policy: some issues arising from research and practice*. Lewes, Falmer Press.

O'Hanlon, C. (1995c) The politics of evaluation: an action research perspective, *Irish Education Studies Journal*, 14: 51–63.

O'Hanlon, C. (1997) The professional journal, genres and personal development in higher education, in S. Hollingsworth (ed.) *International Action Research: A Case Book for Educational Reform*. London: Falmer Press.

Oliver, M. (1996) *Understanding Disability: From Theory to Practice*. London: Macmillan.

Paulin, T. (2002) Vladimir Ilych, in *The Invasion Handbook*. London: Faber and Faber.

Peters, R.S. (1966) *Ethics and Education*. London: George Allen and Unwin.

Pijl, S.J., Meijer, C. and Hegarty, S. (1997) *Inclusive Education: A Global Agenda*. London: Routledge.

Potter, J. and Wetherall, M. (1987) *Discourse and Social Psychology*. London: Sage.

Pring, R. (2000) *Philosophy of Educational Research*. London: Continuum.

Putnamm, R. (1993) The prosperous community: social capital and public life, *American Prospect*, 13, 307–8.

Rawls, J.A. (1971) *Theory of Justice*. Cambridge, MA: Harvard University Press.

Reynolds, D. (1995) *School Effectiveness Research, Policy and Practice*. London: Cassell.

Richardson, P. (2000) *Supporting SENCOs through a Focus on Inclusion*. SENCO Update no. 20. London: Optimus Publishing.

Ricoeur, P. (1970) *Freud and Philosophy: An Essay in Interpretation*. New Haven, CT: Yale University Press.

Rogers, C. (1951) *Student Centered Teaching in Client Centered Therapy*. Boston: Houghton Mifflin.

Rogers, C. and Kutnick, P. (eds) (1990) *The Social Psychology of the Primary School*. London: Routledge.

Rudduck, J. (1985) The improvement of teaching through research, *Cambridge Journal of Education*, 15: 123–7.

Sample, J. and Warland, R. (1973) Attitude and prediction of behaviour, *Social Forces*, 52: 292–303.

Sartre, J.-P. (1957) *Being and Nothingness*. London: Methuen.

Schon, D.A. (1983) *The Reflective Practitioner*. San Francisco: Jossey-Bass.

Schon, D.A. (1987) *Educating the Reflective Practitioner*. San Francisco: Jossey-Bass.

Schulman, J. (1992) *Case Methods in Teacher Education*. New York: Teachers College Press.

Schwab, J.J. (1978) Eros and education: a discussion of one aspect of discussion, in I. Westbury and N.J. Wilof (eds), *Science Curriculum and Liberal Education: Selected Essays*. Chicago: University of Chicago Press.

Sherman, N. (1997) *Making Necessity a Virtue: Aristotle and Kant on Virtue*. Cambridge: Cambridge University Press.

Sikes, P. (1997) *Parents who Teach: Stories from School and from Home*. London: Cassell.

Simons, H. (1987) *Getting to Know Schools in a Democracy*, London: Falmer Press.

Slee, R. (1996) Inclusive education in Australia? Not yet! *Cambridge Journal of Education*, 26(1): 19–32.

Slee, R. (1999) Policies and practices? Inclusive education and its effect on schooling, in H. Daniels and P. Garner (eds) *Inclusive Education: Supporting Inclusion in Education Systems*. London: Kogan Page.

Smith, F. (1986) *Insult to Intelligence: The Bureaucratic Invasion of Our Classrooms*. New York: Arbor House.

Social Exclusion Unit (1998) *Truancy and School Exclusion: Report by the Social Exclusion Unit*. London: HMSO.

Social Justice Commission (1994) *Social Justice: A Report of the Commission on Social Justice*. London: Vintage.

Stenhouse, L. (1975) *An Introduction to Curriculum Research and Development*. London: Heinemann.

Stenhouse, L. (1983) *Authority, Education and Emancipation*. London: Heinemann.

SU (2002) *Senco Update*, 31, London: Optimus.

Tesch, R. (1990) *Qualitative Research: Analysis Types and Software Tools*. London: Falmer Press.

Tickle, L. (1995) Testing for quality in educational action research: a terrifying taxonomy? *Education Action Research Journal*, 3(2): 233–7.

Tomlinson, S. (2000) Ethnic minorities and education: new disadvantages, in T. Cox (ed.) *Combating Educational Disadvantage: Meeting the Needs of Vulnerable Children*. London: Falmer Press.

Troyna, B. and Hatcher, R. (1992) *Racism in Children's Lives*. London: Routledge.

UN (1993) *Standard Rules on the Equalisation of Opportunities for Persons with Disabilities*. New York: United Nations.

UNESCO (1994) *The Salamanca Statement and Framework for Action on Special Needs Education*. Paris: UNESCO.

Udvari, A. and Thousand, J. (1996) Creating a responsive curriculum for inclusive schools, *Remedial and Special Education*, 17(3): 182–92.

Vlachou, A.D. (1997) *Struggles for Inclusive Education: An Ethnographic Study*. Buckingham: Open University Press.

Vygotsky, L.S. (1978) *Mind in Society: The Development of Higher Psychological Processes.* Cambridge, MA: Harvard University Press.

Webb, R. (1990) *Practitioner Research in the Primary School.* Lewes: Falmer Press.

Williams, R. (2000) *Lost Icons: Reflections on Cultural Bereavement.* Edinburgh: T. and T. Clark.

Winter, R. (1989) *Learning from Experience.* London: Falmer Press.

YCS (2001) *Youth Cohort Study: The Activities and Experiences of 19 Year Olds: England and Wales 2000.* London: DfES.

Young, I.M. (1990) *Justice and the Politics of Difference.* Princeton, NJ: Princeton University Press.

Index